W9-ACM-258

SISTER CARRIE

Theodore Dreiser's Sociological Tragedy

TWAYNE'S MASTERWORK STUDIES

Robert Lecker, General Editor

SISTER CARRIE

Theodore Dreiser's Sociological Tragedy

David E. E. Sloane

TWAYNE PUBLISHERS • NEW YORK
Maxwell Macmillan Canada • Toronto
Maxwell Macmillan International • New York   Oxford   Singapore   Sydney

Twayne's Masterwork Studies No. 97

Sister Carrie: Theodore Dreiser's Sociological Tragedy
David E. E. Sloane

Twayne Publishers
Macmillan Publishing Company
866 Third Avenue
New York, New York 10022

Maxwell Macmillan Canada, Inc.
1200 Eglinton Avenue East
Suite 200
Don Mills, Ontario M3C 3N1

Macmillan Publishing Company is part of the Maxwell Communication Group of Companies.

Library of Congress Cataloging-in-Publication Data

Sloane, David E. E., 1943–
    Sister Carrie, Theodore Dreiser's sociological tragedy / David
E.E. Sloane.
        p. cm. — (Twayne's masterwork studies ; no. 97)
    Includes bibliographical references (p.   ) and index.
    ISBN 0-8057-8098-X (alk. paper)—ISBN 0-8057-8554-X (pbk.: alk. paper)
    1. Dreiser, Theodore, 1871–1945. Sister Carrie.   2. Social
problems in literature.   3. Tragic, The, in literature.   I. Title.
II. Series.
PS3507.R55S5935   1992
813'.52—dc20
                                                            92-13516
                                                            CIP

The paper used in this publication meets the minimum requirements of American National Standard for Information Sciences—Permanence of Paper for Printed Library Materials. ANSI Z3948-1984. ⊗ ™

10 9 8 7 6 5 4 3 2 1 (hc)
10 9 8 7 6 5 4 3 2 1 (pb)

Printed in the United States of America

To Rachel and Little David

Contents

Note on the References and Acknowledgments

References to *Sister Carrie* are to the Norton Critical Edition, ed. Donald Pizer (New York: W. W. Norton, 1991 [1970]), and are cited parenthetically in the text. References to the Pennsylvania edition, ed. James L. W. West III (Philadelphia: University of Pennsylvania Press, 1981), which offers an alternate text of the novel including manuscript material not published in the first edition used as the basis for the Norton edition, are cited parenthetically as "Penn."

I am particularly grateful to Thomas P. Riggio, Shelley Fisher Fishkin, and Paul Orlov for reading and commenting on a draft of this manuscript; I also wish to thank Vera Dreiser and my colleagues at the University of New Haven for their kind assistance. The reference librarians at the University of New Haven Library were always helpful in meeting my requests. English Department Chair Paul Marx, Dean Joseph Chepaitis, Provost Alex Sommers, and University of New Haven President Dr. Phillip Kaplan were, as in the past, extremely supportive of my work, and I am grateful to them. Henry Farkas of the university's Computer Resource Center also contributed immeasurable support. The University of New Haven supported this work with a Summer Research Fellowship and other research grants. Last, but by no means least, I am indebted to my students, including Steven Douglas, Nancy Hilton, Rebecca McFarland, and Matt Scinto, for volunteering their good ideas in discussions of *Sister Carrie* in class.

Theodore Dreiser, half-length portrait, about 1900

Published by permission of Van Pelt Library, Special Collections Department, University of Pennsylvania

Chronology:
Theodore Dreiser's
Life and Works

Chronology:
Theodore Dreiser's Life and Works

1871   Herman Theodore Dreiser born to Paul and Mary Schanab
        Dreiser on 27 August in Terre Haute, Indiana, ninth of 10
        children.

1882   Family rescued from utter destitution in Sullivan, Indiana, by
        brother Paul Dresser, succeeding as a minstrel show comedian,
        and a madam with whom he has a temporary liaison.

1883–1887 Family lives in Evansville, Chicago, and Warsaw, Indiana, al-
        ways in difficult circumstances, economically, and outside con-
        ventional social circles, a situation of which Dreiser is keenly
        aware. In Warsaw Dreiser's sexual awakening occurs. His sis-
        ter Emma in Chicago runs off with a thief to New York,
        anticipating Carrie's story, and his sister Mame and, to a lesser
        extent, his sister Sylvia have experiences leading to the story
        of Jennie Gerhardt. *Dawn* (1931) will chronicle this period of
        Dreiser's life.

1889   Attends the University of Indiana for one year, after a former
        teacher locates him clerking for a Chicago dry goods firm and
        offers to pay his tuition.

1890   Mother dies 14 November.

1892   Begins reporting career with the Chicago *Globe* but soon
        moves to the St. Louis *Globe-Democrat* and the St. Louis

Republic. Dreiser will chronicle this period in *Newspaper Days* (1922).

1894   Meets Arthur Henry while working for the Toledo *Blade*; moves to New York.

1895   Begins editing *Ev'ry Month* magazine for Howley-Haviland, a song-publishing company in which his brother Paul Dresser is a principal.

1897   Quits *Ev'ry Month* and begins freelancing, after writing the first verse and chorus of a song that becomes Paul Dresser's smash hit of 1898, "On the Banks of the Wabash."

1898   Marries Sara "Jug" Osborne White, a Missouri schoolteacher he has courted for five years, but with some misgivings about the limitations implied by marriage.

1899   Listed in *Who's Who* as editor, writer, and contributor to several major periodicals. Begins writing *Sister Carrie* with Arthur Henry's encouragement, allowing significant editing of the final draft by Henry and Jug.

1900   *Sister Carrie* published by Doubleday, Page & Co. but is neither advertised nor aggressively distributed because of Frank Doubleday, who sees the book as immoral.

1901   Heinemann publishes a shortened *Sister Carrie* edition in England to moderate praise and sales.

1902   Dreiser has nervous breakdown following *Sister Carrie* suppression in United States. Brother Paul finds him, sends him to a health retreat, and gets him started toward recovery.

1906   Paul Dresser dies of a heart attack 30 January at his sister Emma's home, more or less destitute and friendless at age 46.

1907   B. W. Dodge & Co. republishes *Sister Carrie*; Dreiser changes only one passage, a plagiarism from George Ade, and deletes the acknowledgments to Arthur Henry, from whom he is now estranged; the novel is well reviewed. Dreiser takes job as editor of domestic patternmaker Butterick's magazines and becomes affluent as a result.

1911   *Jennie Gerhardt* published by Harper & Bros., who obtain rights to reprint *Sister Carrie* as part of the negotiation.

1912   *The Financier*, the first volume in Dreiser's "trilogy of desire," chronicles the career of Charles Yerkes; *Sister Carrie* reissued.

1914   *The Titan*, second volume in Dreiser's "trilogy of desire." Dreiser separates from Jug permanently.

1915   *The "Genius,"* a barely disguised autobiography, is published and banned as obscene and blasphemous the following year by the New York Society for the Supression of Vice. It is withdrawn by the publisher and does not reappear until 1923.

1917–1923   The suppression of his novels, a preference by magazine editors for lighter and less tortuous material than he is writing, and his pro-Germanism cause Dreiser to live in relative poverty. Publishes various volumes, including a play and *Free and Other Stories.*

1919   Helen Patges Richardson, an attractive 25-year-old, arrives on Dreiser's doorstep unannounced. They begin a lasting love affair but are not married until 1944, after the death of Jug.

1925   *An American Tragedy,* published as a two-volume set, sells 50,000 sets in a year, and establishes Dreiser as a novelist of major importance in American literature; the novel is banned in Boston. Royalties begin to make Dreiser affluent.

1927   Visits the Soviet Union; the annoyances of the trip do not abate his interest in communism.

1928   *Dreiser Looks at Russia.*

1930   Loses Nobel Prize to Sinclair Lewis by one vote. Lewis in his acceptance speech says that Dreiser more than any other writer has opened the way to honesty and passion in modern fiction.

1931   *Dawn* (autobiography), *Tragic America* (social comment), and *Moods . . . Cadenced and Declaimed* (poetry).

1937   Sister Emma dies.

1945   Dies in Hollywood, California, on 28 December after having joined the Communist party five months earlier.

1946   *The Bulwark.*

1947   *The Stoic* completes the "trilogy of desire."

1952   Movie of *Sister Carrie* made as *Carrie.*

1981   The Pennsylvania edition of *Sister Carrie* offers a radically revised and expanded text of the novel.

LITERARY AND HISTORICAL CONTEXT

1

Toward a Modern America

Although visitors to the Lowell, Massachusetts, mills in the 1840s delighted in the thrift, hunger for education, and idealism of the young women in the mills, the outlook for the American working class was hardly promising by the end of the same century, when sweatshops with their safety and health abuses were making labor unions a workingman's necessity. Hamlin Garland's "Under the Lion's Paw" had boldly stated the farmer's plight, but everyday literature had by no means coped with the life consequences of the development of the great modern factories and urban centers such as Chicago and New York. Working men, and working women even more so, were still depicted in literature as formal, stilted, and moral. Where the burlesquers of the 1870s tirelessly attacked as absurd Whittier's notion in "Maud Muller" that a poor girl might have found happiness by marrying a rich man, many fictional stories showed that poor but honest was as good as high and mighty any time. Theodore Dreiser's family history of poverty and failure, mirroring the history of many other immigrant families, told him that Whittier's vision was unreal. In 1889 Mark Twain's Connecticut Yankee might conjure up a "man factory" and a "new deal" for Arthurian England, but American industrialists

3

worked for the benefit of their shareholders; Commodore Vanderbilt's remark "The public be damned" applied to most industrial workers. The plight of the common American worker had worsened during the "age of shoddy" ushered in by the Civil War. New York's commercial energy seemed to have surpassed Boston's culture, and in the midcontinent, Chicago's mighty energy was establishing a midwestern mythos of commercial giantism—a sense of mythic rawness, power, and promise that was actively nurtured by Chicago's own promoters. Yet the shifting emphasis in American commercial geography may have diminished recognition of the terrible plight of the lowest classes of workers and laborers. At the top of the economic ladder in 1900, the year Andrew Carnegie's share of the profits from his steel mills was $25 million, J. P. Morgan bought Carnegie's mills for $440 million and created the nation's first billion-dollar corporation, U.S. Steel. Lower down the ladder, however, many new immigrants arriving from southern and western Europe were not skilled workers and thus were unable to control their part of the labor market. Their plight was even worse than that of workers unionizing in opposition to the unbridled wage control of capitalist bosses. Their physical circumstances were reduced, their problems were ignored, and they represented a sad outcome of industrialism, which George Pope Morris in the 1840s had praised in an optimistic chant about the future of machines in "The Song of the Sewing Machine":

> Poverty brings no disaster
> Merrily I glide along,
> For no thankless, sordid master,
> Ever seeks to do me wrong.[1]

Sweatshops dominated the lives of the poor; to protect the modern seamstress, the International Ladies' Garment Workers Union (ILGWU) came into being in the same year that Dreiser published his first novel—1900. Jacob Riis in *How the Other Half Lives* (1890) had unhappily documented the abject poverty of the poor in New York; reporters such as the young Theodore Dreiser saw and described those conditions in many cities. *Sister Carrie* is a fictional representation of the moral and economic dilemmas of the urban poor in that era.

Moral questions were as much a matter of concern by 1900 as they were in the 1920s when Henry Ford's mobile living rooms—the ubiquitous black Ford—threatened every flapper with instant seduction, but social critics were even less tolerated in 1900 than they were in the roaring twenties.[2] The suppression of vice was a common practice, needing no defense; but the emphasis was on suppression, not on a change in the social order. Popular newspapers battened on stories of vice and crime, but this factor had been a constant since the Civil War. Nevertheless some American realist writers—who chose not to deal with the fantasy of historical romance or society novels— were increasingly concerned with exploring the physical standing of the individual and finding a means of improving it. Stephen Crane in 1893 had shown a young girl, Maggie, flowering in a mud puddle of corruption, seduced and abandoned; Frank Norris in 1899 had shown the violent primitive urges breaking loose not only in nature but also in a heavy-handed San Francisco dentist named McTeague. Thorstein Veblen in 1899 put forth the concept of "conspicuous consumption" in *The Theory of the Leisure Class*, but he was received coolly.

The Gibson girl was the high ideal, particularly as presented in Gibson's cartoons in *Life*. Her jaded lines in the captions of those same cartoons suggested that self-interest, boredom, and money motivation were all-encompassing attitudes toward marriage and sexual affairs. Such attitudes were tolerated only as long as the outward proprieties were observed; conventions of middle-class morality were bolstered by a variety of institutional forces, some having a quasi-legal authority. Gaudy philanthropic activities and charity balls were a way of life for the ostentatious rich.

Morality and seduction, as embodied in the fallen woman, from revolutionary times, and the white slave trade, after the Civil War, had been significant topics among popular writers. Popular novels also depicted the working girl as an innocent seeking only the highest ideals, particularly marriage, which were consistent with the conventions of success by luck and pluck laid out decades earlier by Horatio Alger, Jr.

George Horace Lorimer was about to initiate a 50-year reign of the ideal of the sentimental rough-but-honest business and working folk in the *Saturday Evening Post*, and popular taste typically gravitated more toward the superficiality of such portraits than toward the naturalist writings of the French school and Norris, Crane, Harold Frederic, and other sterner realists, the school in which Dreiser would soon be the dominant figure. Lorimer's "Old Gorgon Graham" was the crusty but lovable boss, admiring grit and toughness in the young and seeing for them all the economic possibilities they could take on; Graham's supposed "letters" to his son made him the American equivalent of Lord Chesterfield, a man who substitutes business life for manners. Adult counterparts to the juveniles of Alger, the earlier heroes were followed in the 1920–50 era by such cultural icons as "Tugboat Annie," who rescues the lost at sea and ashore without compromising virtue or independence: the spiritual and mental opposite of the reticent Carrie Meeber.[3]

Taken altogether, the economic reality of life in America may have dictated the appearance of a writer such as Dreiser, but the intellectual climate, popular ethics, and social mores did not favor his appeal. His fiction and his prose proved alike difficult, awkward, sometimes intellectually jumbled, and often morally affronting. His characters were the moral opposites of those that gained Lorimer his success. As Shelley Fisher Fishkin points out in the introduction to *From Fact to Fiction*, Dreiser's investigation of economic inequality was self-censored in his journalism but was accepted in his fiction.[4] To earn his own living as a magazine editor in the decade following *Sister Carrie*, in fact, Dreiser sought, presented, and wrote material radically different than that which appeared in his novels. Whereas his documentary realism was admirably suited to an age of newspaper readers, his penchant for questioning moral and sexual assumptions in his novels affronted a rising middle class of church-going Americans. The social context of his fiction presented dogmatists with issues that they did not wish to discuss. Thoughtful foreign readers and some Americans admired the freedom and questioning of social restraint and prejudice that Dreiser represented in his novels, but conventional morality, then as now, required self-denial in the face of seemingly overwhelming inducements to immoral indulgence; Dreiser's challenges in his fiction to what he saw as flagrantly unrealistic depictions of human nature were met by 20 years of attempts to suppress his best work.

2

The Importance of the Work

Sister Carrie is of major importance on five counts. First, it represents an astonishing breakthrough in the presentation of amoral actions by characters estranged from the social and sexual pretenses of their day. Second, its use of common speech is an impressive adjunct to its amoral position and at the time was also considered a breakthrough to a common "real" diction of midwestern America. Third, its repetitious heaping up of minute details, observations, scientific and pseudoscientific reasoning, and even the language of fantasy and melodrama—all in the author's voice—marks a significant departure from the action novels and sentimental romances of its era. Fourth, as a representative of the naturalist or sterner realist school of fiction, the novel provides an array of naturalist technical and philosophic traits, particularly in the grip of natural and physical necessity on the characters, but such traits are mixed unapologetically with a vast number of other images, devices, and sexist clichés lifted from popular fiction. Fifth, and last, *Sister Carrie*'s publishing history—two distinctly different texts are now in print—provides yet another window into American cultural history.

The book posed problems for many readers on moral grounds. The likable characters are immoral; the characters who act according to standard expectations—the Hansons and Julia Hurstwood—are repugnant, even though they adhere to the prevailing morality. Dreiser offers sympathy to the sinners and not only does not judge them harshly but even apologizes for them. Burton Rascoe in pointing out how shocking *Sister Carrie* was, noted that the mild realist Henry Blake Fuller withdrew from writing realistic descriptions of the city after his Chicago novels *The Cliff-Dwellers* (1893) and *With the Procession* (1895) aroused a storm of criticism.[1] Dorothy Dudley, in *Dreiser and the Land of the Free*, adds the story of Frank Doubleday's wife declaring that she would rather mop floors for her livelihood than have her husband's firm publish an immoral book such as *Sister Carrie*.[2] The strength of these stories, apocryphal or not, illustrates the depth of feeling aroused by such a departure in moral portraiture as *Sister Carrie*.

Dreiser's style has also attracted considerable attention. Critics have commented on his extreme awkwardness, pointing out that he even uses words that are literally wrong in context. His reflection of the voice of midwesterners in such phrases as "it ached her" to describe Carrie's feelings may be a strength or a grotesquerie, depending on what sort of fluidity a reader expects in the narration. The obvious mixing of melodramatic language, poetic interjections, harsh dialect, and monotonous reportorial style disconcerted more than one critic and buttressed their antagonism toward the apparently immoral message of the text, itself a mélange of realism, naturalism, and sentimental melodrama, with gobbets of pseudoscience thrown in, as more than one reviewer noted. Dreiser's style as a former newspaper writer may also be part of his awkwardness, for he heaps up details with a newspaperman's love of the literal report. *The Financier* and *An American Tragedy* go considerably further in this direction by depicting the workings of Philadelphia streetcar financing and the widest range of American social experience, but *Sister Carrie* is plainly the forerunner of these novels because it describes the cityscape and the characters of the new urban world. It creates for the first time in American letters the descriptive style defined in chapter 7 of this study as "sociological realism."

Much of the power of *Sister Carrie* lies in its "photographic" depiction of Chicago and New York and in its portrayal of the fall of one of the leaders of this world, Hurstwood. More than one critic has considered the novel an achievement in American literature owing to its faithfulness to detail: clothing, speech, decor, and architectural descriptions all seem to bring us into the world of commerce, industrial grime, and deprivation. Critics have complained that Dreiser records every detail ponderously as if it were about to pass out of existence. Crucial to Dreiser's naturalism, however, is the sense of inevitable factuality and the inescapable process of change in the lives of the characters—change intricately linked to the lives of the characters through the artifacts that engulf them. In this setting-inspired social inevitability the fall of Hurstwood develops. Even though, as critics have written, the novel suffers a "broken back" when Hurstwood replaces Carrie as the center of the novel, it also offers an almost classical tragic ending. The power of *Sister Carrie* may, in fact, partly derive from the power of Hurstwood to take over and represent a component of experience that is not really divorced from Carrie. After finishing the novel the reader's sense of depression may be attributed to being overwhelmed by the conjoined fates of Carrie, Drouet, and Hurstwood, to being convinced that Carrie's life is tragic rather than comic, and to feeling that Dreiser's depiction of the characters as yearning and unhappy in the face of worldly success is wholly accurate.

Finally, the naturalism of the book seems to lead remorselessly to the social and physical decline of George Hurstwood and his death by suicide. Hurstwood's defeat by the world, by his own mistakes, by the violence of the strike, and by the chill of winter are compounded within his own nature by a "drifting" quality that he shares with Carrie and by implication with all mankind. The weaknesses in the personalities of Hurstwood and Carrie are consistent with the psychological concepts newly articulated by William James in the 1890s. The sequence of events marking Hurstwood's decline in conjunction with Carrie's rise is more powerfully expressed than in any published work up to that time. In Dreiser's later novels sexual desire and the thrust of circumstances become even more pronounced themes. Dreiser approaches modern existentialism at the end of *The Financier*, further examines sexuality and the yielding human nature in *Jennie Gerhardt* and *The "Genius,"* and provides the massive documentary realism of *An American Tragedy,* finally bringing together all the themes of sexual drive, social need, and emotional/intellectual yearning in one figure, Clyde Griffiths, Carrie's ultimate successor.

3

Critical Reception

Even before it was published, Dreiser's manuscript received a stunning and enthusiastic endorsement from Frank Norris, a reader for Doubleday and Page and the young dean of the emerging naturalists, whose novel *McTeague* many critics believed brought a stronger coarser naturalism into American fiction. Norris's urgency about the novel's importance contributed to the problems surrounding the book's publication, for in the absence of the senior partner, Frank Doubleday, the junior partner Page gave Dreiser a strong verbal endorsement of the novel before Dreiser had an actual written contract. When Doubleday decided, on close reading of the proofs, that he did not want his firm associated with the novel because it was too "immoral," Dreiser's friend Arthur Henry urged Dreiser to insist on publication, and Norris concurred. Subsequently, a mere 558 copies were bound, and no effort was made to promote the book, virtually killing it despite Norris's wide distribution of review copies among newspapers. Fewer than 500 copies of the initial printing were sold. As early as 1902 stories circulated about the suppression of the novel.

Every reader of the manuscript recognized its lack of "delicacy," a comment that appeared in the manuscript's first review from the publishing firm Harper's. Arthur Henry, Sara Osborne White, known as "Jug," and Dreiser took pains to edit the text of a number of improprieties, the power of which was suggested when the typists of the original manuscript sent a note to Dreiser to hurry and send them more of his "iniquitous" novel soon.[1] Further editing by Doubleday also may have occurred, which accounts for the interest of the major reconstruction effort undertaken by the editors of the Pennsylvania edition of 1981. Many cuts were made merely to shorten a bulky manuscript, but several sleazy minor characters and incidents were dropped. The British edition of 1901 was further cut and was a third shorter than the American edition, with all the cuts coming from the first 200 pages. When Dreiser was preparing to print the 1907 Dodge edition, however, he altered only the single page in the 1900 edition on which he plagiarized George Ade's portrait of a masher in describing Drouet. No cuts were restored, and even in later reprintings of the novel that required resetting type the 1907 text was perpetuated.

The 1900–1901 reviews are a mixed bag, as Jack Salzman's *Theodore Dreiser: The Critical Reception* suggests in the comprehensive selection of reviews it reprints.[2] Major American literary journals did not review *Sister Carrie*. *Atlantic Monthly*, *North American Review*, *Critic*, and several others were notably silent. A number of newspaper reviews, a result of Frank Norris's distribution of review copies, took a wide range of approaches to the novel, anticipating the critical problems that have occupied scholars ever since. The (Omaha) *Daily Bee* noted that "It is not a book to be put into the hands of every reader indiscriminately."[3] The reader in New Haven mentioned Balzac, and in Chicago, Zola was cited in the *Times-Herald* review, which called Dreiser's book "in its field, a great American novel."[4] *The Interior* noted that the book was a bit of "modern realism which does several notable things in a slovenly manner," raising the question of style as did many other critics.[5] It went on to notice the lack of moral robustness in the drifting Carrie and the weak moral stamina of Hurstwood, but it clearly identified the importance of the novel's portraiture by concluding that the reviewer would await another book from Dreiser with impatience. Other reviewers, however, were not so kind. *Life*, the humor magazine that had rejected *Huckleberry Finn* as coarse in 1885, sniped that girls who imagine they can follow in Carrie's footsteps will end on "the Island" or in the gutter;[6] and the reviewer for the (Pittsburgh) *Commercial Gazette* sneered that Carrie's decision to get something to wear rather than support Hurstwood showed the novelist's grasp of "woman nature."[7] Others found the book inept in style, too long, or too "unhealthful in tone" to merit interest. The attacks on the book's immorality probably stung Dreiser the most.

William Marion Reedy of the (St. Louis) *Mirror* wrote one of the most perceptive reviews. Agreeing that the novel was not a "nice" novel but a "story of the seamy side," he declared that its "veritism out-Howells Mr. Howells and out-Garlands Mr. Hamlin Garland."[8] Even though Carrie's fall is "a fall upwards," Reedy considered the novel "very much restrained," but he also saw the underlying meaning of the novel very clearly: "And there grows upon the reader the impression that there lurks behind the mere story an intense, fierce resentment of the conditions glimpsed." Finally, Reedy described Hurstwood's fall as demonstrating Dreiser's "real power" (in Salzman, 7). Thus, Reedy identified much of importance that later critics have discussed in the novel; he penetrates to the emotion haunting Dreiser's sense of poverty and the economic forces controlling human desire. W. A. Swanberg, in his biography *Dreiser*, writes that the reviews of *Sister Carrie* were negative and put a damper on the enthusiasm of Frank Norris, who was eagerly promoting the work.[9] Yet many balanced appraisals of the book anticipated criticisms of the novel that continue to this day, even though later reviews accept the book's status as a modern American classic. Nevertheless a few negative words such as describing the novel as "too realistic," "depressing," or "commonplace," or an overall impression as leaving a "bad taste," show the power of newspaper reviews to destroy book sales. No popular readership materialized, and the broader literary circle did not see reviews in the more elevated periodicals. The book was sent to bookstores only by request, and without publicity, so chance sales were impossible. Thus, Dreiser's sense that his book was treated unfairly by the press and the publisher seems fully justified.

British publications reviewed a novel shortened by Dreiser and Arthur Henry to 120 pages less than the American edition. The Heinemann edition was meant to fit the size of Heinemann's "Dollar Library," and cuts made in the first 200 pages shortened Carrie's story but left the last part of the novel intact. The major British journals, unlike their American counterparts, did review *Sister Carrie* with enthusiasm, and most found Hurstwood's fall to be a dominating element. The (London) *Daily Mail* said, "At last a really strong novel has come from America," and the (Manchester) *Guardian* commented that *Sister Carrie* was "faithful, acute, unprejudiced, and it should belong to the veritable 'documents' of American history."[10] The *Guardian* winced at Dreiser's Americanisms but praised his scientific portraiture and his refusal to idealize his characters. The *Academy*'s reviewer confessed to having been "startled into interest" by the description of Carrie as an American heroine: "The book is thoroughly good, alike in accurate and sympathetic observation, in human sympathy, in lyric appeal, and in dramatic power."[11] Theodore Watts-Dunton, in the distinguished pages of the *Athenaeum*, thought that the book could stand beside Zola's *Nana*, "typical, both, in the faults of its manner and in the wealth and diversity of its matter, of the great country which gave it birth."[12] He noted in the novel's language the vernacular of the streets and bars and seemed to dislike the manner of the book, but he found "no single note of unreality. . . . It is untrammeled by any single concession to convention or tradition, literary or social" (in Salzman, 23). It was particularly on the basis of such British reviews that an American underground readership developed, paving the way for a much more thoughtful reception of the 1907 Dodge edition.

The 1907 Dodge reprint drew many more significant reviews from the major American journals. The (New Orleans) *Picayune* found Dreiser more important than Howells because he deals with elemental passions as well as the pettiness of human nature, and better than Edith Wharton because he embraces "the great mean of human nature" rather than a narrow class.[13] Dreiser had been friendly with Joseph Horner Coates, editor of the Philadelphia *Era*, for several years, calling on him in Philadelphia during his nervous breakdown period and selling him items for the *Era*. Coates responded by reviewing *Sister Carrie* in the October 1907 *North American Review*, probably leaning for insights on his talks with Dreiser. Noting the novel's peculiarly individual power, the "virile earnestness and serious purpose," as had other critics, Coates went on to praise the delicacy with which Dreiser treated Carrie's career, which to Coates enforced "a moral lesson"— although Coates did not say that a moral lesson other than the conventional one might have been intended.[14] More important, Coates stated that the novel's title was "no doubt, intended to suggest the kinship of the world" (in Salzman, 52), a suggestion that Thomas Riggio has put forth elsewhere in discussing the genesis of the heroine.[15] Coates wrote, "the economic change in industrial conditions is more and more bringing all humanity into closer touch; with the result that the high and mighty influence, as never before, the desires and the ambitions, and the passions, too, of those who are low in degree" (in Salzman, 53). The "racial crises"—the broad social development of western man—as thus interpreted in Coates's review provide a remarkable gloss on all of Dreiser's novels through *An American Tragedy*. Such a review gives us a philosophical framework within which Carrie's rise and Hurstwood's fall make great and inevitable sense. Of course, even in 1907, the controversy over *Sister Carrie* raged on; the (Akron) *Journal* of 30 November 1907 cried out, "The book is a dangerous one, the story of lives steeped in sin and degradation. . . . The whole thing is immoral and disgusting."[16]

One of the most ringing attacks on Dreiser's canon came in 1915 when one of America's leading critics, Stuart P. Sherman, cannonaded Dreiser's novels in an article entitled "The Barbaric Naturalism of Mr. Dreiser" in *The Nation*. Sherman's position sheds further light on the divergence in underlying philosophies between Dreiser's praisers and his detractors. Sherman found no moral value and no beauty in Dreiser's work. Each of Dreiser's books from *Sister Carrie* on was seen as a "ferocious argument" in favor of a few brutal generalizations that reduced the problem of the novelist to the lowest possible terms.[17] Sherman finally argued that Dreiser, like Zola, should be called a naturalist, not a realist, because his work was based on a theory and selling him items for the *Era*. Coates responded by reviewing *Sister Carrie* in the October 1907 *North American Review*, probably leaning for insights on his talks with Dreiser. Noting the novel's peculiarly individual power, the "virile earnestness and serious purpose," as had other critics, Coates went on to praise the delicacy with which Dreiser treated Carrie's career, which to Coates enforced "a moral lesson"— although Coates did not say that a moral lesson other than the conventional one might have been intended.[14] More important, Coates stated that the novel's title was "no doubt, intended to suggest the kinship of the world" (in Salzman, 52), a suggestion that Thomas Riggio has put forth elsewhere in discussing the genesis of the heroine.[15] Coates wrote, "the economic change in industrial conditions is more and more bringing all humanity into closer touch; with the result that the high and mighty influence, as never before, the desires and the ambitions, and the passions, too, of those who are low in degree" (in Salzman, 53). The "racial crises"—the broad social development of western man—as thus interpreted in Coates's review provide a remarkable gloss on all of Dreiser's novels through *An American Tragedy*. Such a review gives us a philosophical framework within which Carrie's rise and Hurstwood's fall make great and inevitable sense. Of course, even in 1907, the controversy over *Sister Carrie* raged on; the (Akron) *Journal* of 30 November 1907 cried out, "The book is a dangerous one, the story of lives steeped in sin and degradation. . . . The whole thing is immoral and disgusting."[16]

One of the most ringing attacks on Dreiser's canon came in 1915 when one of America's leading critics, Stuart P. Sherman, cannonaded Dreiser's novels in an article entitled "The Barbaric Naturalism of Mr. Dreiser" in *The Nation*. Sherman's position sheds further light on the divergence in underlying philosophies between Dreiser's praisers and his detractors. Sherman found no moral value and no beauty in Dreiser's work. Each of Dreiser's books from *Sister Carrie* on was seen as a "ferocious argument" in favor of a few brutal generalizations that reduced the problem of the novelist to the lowest possible terms.[17] Sherman finally argued that Dreiser, like Zola, should be called a naturalist, not a realist, because his work was based on a theory

British publications reviewed a novel shortened by Dreiser and Arthur Henry to 120 pages less than the American edition. The Heinemann edition was meant to fit the size of Heinemann's "Dollar Library," and cuts made in the first 200 pages shortened Carrie's story but left the last part of the novel intact. The major British journals, unlike their American counterparts, did review *Sister Carrie* with enthusiasm, and most found Hurstwood's fall to be a dominating element. The (London) *Daily Mail* said, "At last a really strong novel has come from America," and the (Manchester) *Guardian* commented that *Sister Carrie* was "faithful, acute, unprejudiced, and it should belong to the veritable 'documents' of American history."[10] The *Guardian* winced at Dreiser's Americanisms but praised his scientific portraiture and his refusal to idealize his characters. The *Academy*'s reviewer confessed to having been "startled into interest" by the description of Carrie as an American heroine: "The book is thoroughly good, alike in accurate and sympathetic observation, in human sympathy, in lyric appeal, and in dramatic power."[11] Theodore Watts-Dunton, in the distinguished pages of the *Athenaeum*, thought that the book could stand beside Zola's *Nana*, "typical, both, in the faults of its manner and in the wealth and diversity of its matter, of the great country which gave it birth."[12] He noted in the novel's language the vernacular of the streets and bars and seemed to dislike the manner of the book, but he found "no single note of unreality. . . . It is untrammeled by any single concession to convention or tradition, literary or social" (in Salzman, 23). It was particularly on the basis of such British reviews that an American underground readership developed, paving the way for a much more thoughtful reception of the 1907 Dodge edition.

The 1907 Dodge reprint drew many more significant reviews from the major American journals. The (New Orleans) *Picayune* found Dreiser more important than Howells because he deals with elemental passions as well as the pettiness of human nature, and better than Edith Wharton because he embraces "the great mean of human nature" rather than a narrow class.[13] Dreiser had been friendly with Joseph Horner Coates, editor of the Philadelphia *Era*, for several years, calling on him in Philadelphia during his nervous breakdown period

McTeague almost immediately after, rather than before he finished *Carrie*, this is a general statement rather than a specific source suggestion.

Dreiser would never publish the uniform edition for which he longed, although such lesser figures as Irwin S. Cobb, Frank R. Stockton, and Eugene Field attained that goal. But in 1925 *An American Tragedy* established Dreiser as one of the great writers of the twentieth century. Humanists throughout the 1940s, including such major critics as Lionel Trilling, who published an essay on Dreiser in *The Liberal Imagination* (1945), continued to reject his work as overly materialistic. Alfred Kazin and Charles Shapiro's *The Stature of Theodore Dreiser*, published by the Indiana University Press in 1955, offers a valuable and reasonably comprehensive spread of criticism up to that point, including essays by Mencken, Trilling, Randolph Bourne, and C. C. Walcutt.

The first of the modern scholarly studies was Robert H. Elias's *Theodore Dreiser: Apostle of Nature* (1949), published by the University of Pennsylvania Press, written with Dreiser's cooperation. The press itself has continued to be a seminal publisher of Dreiser material, and Dreiser's papers are at the University of Pennsylvania Library, although the "Carrie" manuscript, a present to H. L. Mencken, is at the New York Public Library. F. O. Matthiessen in *Theodore Dreiser*, the second of the scholarly studies, sees *Carrie* as being outside the realm of conventional novels of its day because it is an accumulation of the facts of the existence that Dreiser had lived up to the writing of the novel.[21] William Wyler may have felt the same way when he made the film of *Sister Carrie* as *Carrie* in 1952 for Paramount, with Jennifer Jones as Carrie and Laurence Olivier as Hurstwood. Reviewing the movie *Carrie* in the *Nation*, Manny Farber complained that all the characters had been made into either national or local types who loved to overact uncharming traits.[22] Drouet sounded like a social worker; camera angles and shallow scene close-ups threw the movie at the spectator. The latter distressing characteristics may also account for the survival of the movie in a few college film classes—and virtually nowhere else. Dreiser's popularity waned in the forties and fifties because he joined the Communist party and partly because his ponderous style seemed a throwback to a previous generation—a criticism that echoed ideas that had first been broached in the original reviews of *Sister Carrie*. In compensation, other major scholarly works on Dreiser were published, and Dreiser's recognition has risen again. The most important works include W. A. Swanberg's *Dreiser*, accepted as the standard biography, and Richard Lingeman's *Theodore Dreiser: At the Gates of the City, 1871–1907*, the first volume of a projected multivolume study of Dreiser, comprehensive and detailed in linking Dreiser to his cultural milieu.[23]

Dreiser has also reaped two major critical assessments, in addition to a vast array of scholarly essays and the *Dreiser Newsletter*, that clearly place *Carrie* centrally in the canon of modern American fiction: Donald Pizer's *The Novels of Theodore Dreiser: A Critical Study* and Ellen Moers's *Two Dreisers*, a close study of *Sister Carrie* and *An American Tragedy*.[24] Modern approaches to Dreiser still wrestle with the original questions; they find far more subtlety in Dreiser's intentions and his conscious use of an awkward style, although even this analysis of his style was hinted at by perceptive early readers.

Finally, the University of Pennsylvania Press edition of *Sister Carrie* published in 1981 gives the novel its due as a target of major scholarly inquiry because the press took on the quest—controversial in itself—for a perfected and fully annotated text. Large chunks of material deleted in the manuscript are added to the printed text for the first time. The changes substantially alter Hurstwood and Drouet's nature; chapter titles are removed because they were presumably not of Dreiser's making or intention; and three possible endings are provided. Chapter numbers are expanded from the original published version to accommodate newly added material from the original typescript. The bulk of this material, crossed out in typescript and now reinterpolated, was not part of the historical record of past reviews and criticism and is thus subject to debate in its own right. The extensive discussion of the text in the Pennsylvania edition and Alfred Kazin's brief introduction to the Penguin Classic edition of the Pennsylvania text (shorn of notes and textual commentary) bring the discussion of the novel as a classic up to the 1980s. Further synthetic texts are proposed to remedy deficiencies in the Pennsylvania edition. Thus, significant discussion of the text will continue in the future; a major university press will soon bring out a volume of new critical essays on the novel, and perhaps some American publisher will risk retrieving the text of the 1901 Heinemann abridgment and reprint it, as was done in the early 1960s.

4

Influences and Echoes

Dreiser's personal history figures in *Sister Carrie* almost as much as does the history of the later nineteenth century. As improbable as the rise of Carrie seems, the career of Theodore Dreiser was equally improbable. The seeming sentimentalities were lived out in parallel experiences of Theodore Dreiser. Hungry children gathering coal on the railroad tracks to warm their impoverished family—as Dreiser and his sisters did; the old-maid midwestern school teacher who identifies genius in one of her students and pays his way to college—as Dreiser's teacher Mildred Fielding did—are clichés. Only an absurd fantasy of fiction writing would permit an author to write his title at the top of a page, sitting across from a friend setting out to write a novel at the same time, and continue to write what would become within no more than a year one of the great American novels. Yet Dreiser claimed that sitting across the table from Arthur Henry as Henry began the manuscript that would become *A Princess of Arcady*, he wrote "Sister Carrie" at the top of the page and then began his novel.

The Fielding incident is improbable enough to merit recounting in any study of Dreiser. Mildred Fielding had been Dreiser's teacher in high school and recognized in him a special gift. In the summer of

1889, after Dreiser had moved to Chicago and become a clerk, he was called to the front office of Hibbard, Spencer, Bartlett & Co., where he was a stock boy at $5 a week. His former teacher had become principal of a Chicago school and had searched out Dreiser to send him, at her expense, to Indiana University. He attended for a year but subsequently rejected Miss Fielding's offer to pay for more schooling because he was lonely and felt out of place. He later wrote that he was irritated by the deprivations experienced by a college student who lacked the money to join fully in college life.[1] So even at this date the gulf between rich and poor and the improbabilities of chance and opportunity seem written larger in Dreiser's life than in the common run of experience.

A study of the various biographies of Dreiser suggests that this one event is not wholly out of place in the run of Dreiser's experience up to 1900. The family was rescued by his brother Paul, who Americanized his last name to "Dresser" to avoid a connection with recent immigrant experience. A showman and minstrel singer, Paul adored his family and came to their rescue with more financial support following his Broadway success. Dreiser's family was extremely poor, close to starvation at several points, and driven into desperate living circumstances. Paul was their miraculous salvation. It was Paul who once appeared to rescue the family from abject poverty, financed by a madam with whom he was cohabiting. He provided considerable and crucial financial help to Theodore, Emma, and others.

Paul's feelings and sentimental comedy were his hallmark. They may have been derived from the kindliness of his impoverished mother, but whatever the source he transmuted his feelings into popular ballads that achieved tremendous success in his time. Paul the songwriter was famous for his sentimental songs such as "The Green Goods Man" and, especially, "On the Banks of the Wabash," with its nostalgia for home. Paul Dresser represents a wide sentimental strain of American culture lying behind Dreiser's life. Perhaps not so incidentally in light of Dreiser's more generalized sympathy toward humanity, various stories suggest that Theodore wrote the first verse of the Wabash song at Paul's prompting in the offices of Howley-Haviland where Dreiser was editor of *Ev'ry Month* magazine. Paul then finished the song and it made him as famous as that other great Indiana poet, James Whitcomb Riley.

Sensual, emotional, comic, and profligate out of immense kindness and sympathy, Paul represented all the attitudes of popular American culture that Dreiser had most trouble equating with conventional social and moral rectitude. Paul, however, strongly encouraged Theodore at crucial points in his early life and established him in the New York publishing world. After Paul's death in 1906, Theodore took the songwriter's piano and had it made into his writing desk, one possession he kept faithfully for the rest of his life.

Dreiser's estimate of his brother's character may figure in his depiction of *Sister Carrie*'s chief male figures Drouet and Hurstwood as spiritually weak and indecisive characters, although the story of L. A. Hopkins provided the precedent for Hurstwood's decline. Paul was a hail-fellow-well-met type who was at home in his element with money and success on Broadway. Theodore, however, thought him shallow and may well have speculated on what a fall from status would have meant to his brother. Theodore suspected that Paul's success as comedian and vaudevillian was a quick and tenuous wealth haphazardly gained from a superficial world. Dreiser's essay "My Brother Paul" depicts Paul much as the novel had depicted Drouet: "He perhaps most suggests Jack Falstaff, with his love of women, his bravado and bluster and his innate good nature and sympathy."[2] When Paul had money, he spent it so freely as to upset Theodore's nagging anxiety about poverty, but Paul's reasons were based on a broadly Dreiserian sympathy that was to be captured in his brother's novels: "You don't know what pulls people down. . . . It's thoughtlessness, or trying to be happy" (*Twelve Men*, 85). Dreiser's conclusion about Paul was that "with a more rugged quality of mind" he might have been less fatally chilled by the icy blasts of human difficulty (*Twelve Men*, 105). The language Dreiser uses in this essay is so suggestive of the language and ideas of *Sister Carrie* that Paul's life suggests the flashing rings and crystal glitter of Hurstwood at his most eminent. Dreiser's foreboding about Paul's character accurately projected his fate as the stuff of

Dreiser's fiction. The interplay of the sentimental and the realistic is so pronounced in the style of the novel that some special consideration may be its stimulus; Paul represents such a possible stimulus.

A second notable component of Dreiser's background that influenced the novel was his sister Emma's adventures in her various love affairs. One obviously significant event is Sister Emma's elopement with L. A. Hopkins, a Chicago saloon clerk who stole $3,500 from his employer Chapin & Gore, abandoned a wife and teenage daughter, and removed himself and Emma to New York. Hopkins later returned the money, according to newspaper accounts, with a letter suggesting the possibility of future reinstatement, but he ended in decline in New York City. Paul and Theodore eventually contrived for Emma to disappear from his life by moving her a few blocks away to a new apartment.[3]

The name "Carrie" itself may have held a host of associations for Dreiser before he began the book. Sister Emma and Dreiser's other sisters had somewhat adventurous sexual histories. Thomas Riggio, in discussing the origins of the novel's Sister Carrie, suggests not only that the title shows the influence of Balzac's family chronicles, which Dreiser may well have had in mind, but also that some real women in Dreiser's history may have shaped the heroine. Sister Emma, of course, signed her letters to the family "Sister Emma" and acted out the love affair that lies at the base of the plot. In addition, a Carrie or "Cad" was a schoolmate of Dreiser's, and Dreiser's comments, suppressed in the book *Dawn*, suggest that she was in some ways sexually provocative to him, as Professor Riggio documents in a study of the original manuscripts relating to that text. Finally, Carrie's personality includes a component of the dreamer and theatrical seeker that partly relates to Dreiser's disposition. She became a star through the same sort of chances that occurred when brother Paul transformed a friend's daughter—Louise Kerlin—into a successful vaudeville actress under the family stage name of Louise Dresser.[4] Sister Emma's life turned downward, her physical appearance deteriorated into dumpy middle-age, but the story of Louise Dresser provides the upward track onto which Dreiser grafted the tale of Emma and Hopkins.

Dreiser's journalism added other strands of background that fit into the creative context of *Sister Carrie*. Poverty had drawn his interest from early in his career, and he gradually elaborated a philosophy of spiritual disintegration around this interest. His article on the life of derelicts printed as "The Curious Shifts of the Poor" in *Demorest's Family Magazine*[5] supplied the description of Hurstwood's decline in the late chapters of the novel when he stands among other fallen men waiting for a flophouse bed. Dreiser's renderings of the strange "Captain" finding beds for the homeless and of New York's first breadline were incorporated in the novel almost directly to represent one of Dreiser's underlying themes, that many of the wealthy are only saved from dereliction by a few favorable chances: "The livid-faced dyspeptic who rides from his club . . . should awaken the same pity as the shivering applicant for a free bed . . . for the ignorance and error that cause the distress of the world."[6]

Dreiser's encounters with famous people provided him with ideas for characterizations. Elmer Gates and Thomas Edison inspired Dreiser to create Ames, who represents another rung in the ladder of Carrie's progression beyond Drouet and Hurstwood. For Dreiser the inventors represented the power of scientific imagination to separate itself from the more materialistic yearnings of the world. In them Dreiser saw a force parallel to the artistic force that he might have been beginning to feel within himself, and that Carrie's emotions represent for her, even though these emotions are not fully under her own control. To skip ahead beyond the composition of *Sister Carrie*, it might be called a mere fact of history that Carrie Meeber's rise from man to man and the emergence of Carrie Madenda as an object of desire precedes rather than follows Norma Jean Dougherty's becoming screen star Marilyn Monroe, the wife of sports hero Joe Dimaggio, and later the wife of playwright intellectual Arthur Miller—prior to succumbing to the longing and despair leading to her suicide.[7] Life mimics art in this instance, but similar cases of a rise to stardom from poor origins occurred and were featured in popular magazines even before *Sister Carrie* was composed.

More broadly, the didactic statements that abound in Dreiser's novel were based on ideas widely promoted in the later nineteenth century. The major recognized font of naturalist philosophy, Herbert Spencer, was one such source, adapting Darwinian evolutionary theories to the competitive social and economic forces roughly defined as capitalism. Dreiser stated such ideas in his editorial pieces for *Ev'ry Month* magazine in 1896 and 1897 and in short stories such as "McEwen of the Shining Slave Makers," a story that incidentally demonstrates that Dreiser, when he chose, could write clean, dynamic, action-oriented fiction. More common sources exist as well. Even such a commonplace manual of everyday life as *Hill's Manual of Social and Business Forms* by Thomas E. Hill helps illuminate the odd ease with which Drouet seduces Carrie.[8] The predicament of an innocent girl is suggested when Hill offers up such forms of social discourse as a model note for a young lady to accept or decline a declaration of love at first sight from an unsolicited suitor (Hill, 113). Dreiser is known to have read *Hill's Manual* as one of his earliest books (Lingeman, 45), and it indeed counsels, under the heading "Kindness to the Erring," a philosophy that suggests a central idea put forth in *Sister Carrie*:

> While error must be deplored and virtue ever commended, we should deal carefully and considerately with the erring, ever remembering that a myriad of untoward circumstances are continually weaving a network around the individual, fettering and binding a soul that otherwise would be white and pure. . . . But while there are those who are apparently exempt from temptation, all are not so fortunate in ability, in strength of purpose and in power of will which may enable them to resist evil. Some are liable to easily err, and it may take, possibly, but a trivial circumstance to carry them aside. (Hill, 182)

The passage prefigures Dreiser's acceptance of Carrie's plight; other passages in *Hill's Manual* are similar. Dreiser's novel, in fact, is a dramatic illustration of the "kindness to the erring" precept from *Hill's Manual*, a social proposition that was current for decades before *Carrie*. Dreiser's critics, of course, were by no means so flexible in their acceptance of the erring.

The antiseduction and antivice literature of the period spoke warningly of the bright saloons and cafés—the very places that Drouet and Hurstwood represent. But Dreiser veered off in his own direction, for morality was not the basis of his opposition to the lure of the lights. Nevertheless, Dreiser's depiction of such dens tells us a lot about the origins of his rhetoric. Col. Dick Maple's *"He Demons"* . . . and . . . *"She Devils"* lectures about "the demon hand of greedy wealth exposed, red with the hearts blood of toil" to recognize "Hell, Harlotism and High-life symbolic and twin sisters."[9] Col. Maple's descriptions could almost be models for Dreiser's rhetoric at a number of points in *Sister Carrie*, even including Dreiser's use of lighting as an indicator of wealth:

> When the lights flash, and cast fantastic shadows upon the streets at Christmas tide this winter, and you and your babies are making merry in anticipation of the joyous time you are to have, Oh stop for a moment in your mad rush of buying, and scrutinize the face of the dear girl who is waiting upon you, who was once "somebody's darling" and inquire of her if she too is happy. Ask her if a bright fire awaits her on her return from her hard day's labor; ask her if a loving father and mother is out tonight piling up pleasant surprises for her on Christmas morn? Ask her if the escutcheon of her conscience is as pure as that great stretch of spotless white is, that blankets the earth? Ask her if every sigh of the wind does not bring before her a panorama of bright days and joyous Christmas times, left desolate by the ghoul like deed of some demon who stabbed to death her every ambition and tore from her warm embrace everything that is near and dear to women—virtue? (Maple, 63)

In some places Dreiser outstrips such passages and in others maintains the problem posed here in slightly downplayed rhetoric, as when the voice of conventional virtue chides Carrie on her fall in chapter 10 (70). Incidentally, Maple, in his chapter on "Fallen Girls and Why They Fall," goes on to point out what Dreiser also demonstrates— that low wages are the chief agent of sin. Col. Maple writes: "In Chicago there are nine thousand girls in the department stores alone, not including the thousands in offices, factories and restaurants; other cities have a like number in proportion to their size. More than fifty per cent of the girls work for a mere pittance, and of course are expected to board and clothe themselves" (Maple, 261). Like Dreiser, Col. Maple commands, "No work should be done that does not give the worker life and comfort" (Maple, 262). Such statements suggest that Dreiser was not alone in his ideology, and Maple's ideas appear socially advanced in comparison to the viewpoints of such critics as Stuart P. Sherman, previously discussed. In fact, Col. Maple's description of seduction corresponds to Drouet's practice, except the process that Maple describes takes place at a Chicago department store counter (Maple, 265–67). He identifies the details of the shopgirl's mean apartment, her lonely life, and the good meal, leading in Maple's elaboration to the villain's drugging the girl into white slavery at a place called "Carrie's." The ideas Dreiser fictionalized resonated on many levels of American culture.

Scholarly studies of fiction of the period directly preceding *Sister Carrie* have further expanded our sense of how much Dreiser's first novel drew on aspects of popular culture. Cathy and Arnold Davidson, in their excellent article "Carrie's Sisters: The Popular Prototypes of Dreiser's Heroine,"[10] have shown convincingly how indebted Dreiser was to novels and novelists of the period immediately preceding *Carrie*, and not merely to the better ones such as those of Stephen Crane, to whom Dreiser is known to have made an occasional reference. The Davidsons note that Dreiser was intensely aware of novelists such as Bertha Clay and Laura Jean Libbey, purveyors of sentimental urban and working-class romances. Unlike the obvious best-sellers of the turn of the century, such as the medieval *Graustark* and the historical *Alice of Old Vincennes*, the novels of Clay and Libbey deal with the social world that Dreiser was attempting to describe, and they deal with it in terms not very different from those Dreiser would use, but Clay and Libbey make use of a radically different set of values in depicting that life and its implications. Typically, the sentimentalists show poor but honest farm girls and working girls discovered by upper-class lovers and rescued from their poverty.

The Davidsons note in "Carrie's Sisters" that Dreiser inverts a number of the sentimental conventions in his novel. Specifically, he takes the "working girl" novel and instead of predicting a lover's intervention, rescue, and redemption shows that being a working girl offers no hope even from melodramatic intervention. Instead of "escaping a fate worse than death," as the Davidsons find Little Leafy doing in Laura Jean Libbey's *Little Leafy, The Cloakmaker's Daughter: A Romantic Story of a Lovely Working-Girl in the City of New York* (1891), Carrie benefits from that worse fate. Carrie is not a pastoral beauty like the conventional heroine but rather gains in looks as she is sexually compromised (Davidson and Davidson, 396–99).

Dreiser was influenced by a second kind of novel, the "costume romance," which preached the gospel of wealth as first laid out by Horatio Alger, Jr., according to which virtue is rewarded and vice is punished. But Dreiser has Carrie fall and succeed, thus mocking the Alger tradition. Bertha M. Clay had further advanced the idea of easy wealth through romance, the Davidsons note, in *Dora Thorne* (1883), which Carrie read and Ames later rejected as bad writing. Dreiser sent *Dora Thorne* to Mencken as a joke 15 years after he wrote *Carrie* and marveled in his autobiography in 1922 that he could have read, and apparently read assiduously, such "sentiment and mush" (Davidson, 407, quoting from *A Book about Myself*). A "logical extension of the success ethic," the Davidsons add, has Carrie moving up the scale of men, while Dreiser questions not only marriage as an institution but also marriages such as the Hurstwoods' and others' (Davidson and Davidson, 405) that are both hypocritical and ugly in many aspects, and hardly the stuff of romance or sentiment.

The Horatio Alger success ethic is inverted in Dreiser. As the Davidsons note, any possibility of Carrie's escape through success is denied, for her brother-in-law Sven Hanson even objects to Carrie's looking out the doorway of their flat. As a working girl in a factory Carrie is subjected not to admiration but rather to crudely sexual overtures. This inversion of the success ethic covers all of Dreiser's characters quite reasonably. Relationships sour and individuals change according to constants of socioeconomic life. Dreiser's view of human potential derives from the world he first encountered as a journalist in

St. Louis, Chicago, and New York and not from the ideal of sudden social elevation as a reward for virtuous suffering or abstinence. Dreiser expands this principle, we note, in the character of Hurstwood, who fails through a certain innate gloominess that chance does not reverse. Dreiser's characters do not rise above the coarser elements of human nature. In a notebook entry in 1903 Dreiser argues that bad luck and the grossness of human existence are universal—common to both the poor and the rich:

> Men, working men . . . ignorant, leading grimy narrow lives—oh I know how they fight and quarrel among themselves. I know too full well that they drink and carouse and are like other men, low and corrupt and mean. Are they not like other men? Are they not like the men who oppress them? Is Morgan pure, is Baer clean? Have they tender hearts, noble souls, fine and beautiful lives? They have money and fine clothes and a pleasant atmosphere of comforts and refinements to move in, but some men are born to degradation and the fault is not theirs after all.[11]

Hurstwood's degradation under his changed circumstances derives naturally from such a philosophy; in fact, Hurstwood represents the very principle implied in the commonality of human circumstances. Dreiser elevates Hurstwood from a mere *maître d'hôtel* to a position of wealth and status so that his character can share J. P. Morgan's role as an oppressor. When Hurstwood experiences adversity, Dreiser can demonstrate how close are the seeming successes of the arrogant rich to the failures of the hopeless poor. Dreiser only spares Hurstwood the last element of degradation—the reputed alcoholism of L. A. Hopkins. Dreiser's sense of tragic art may have intervened, for Hurstwood's attempt to battle natural, social, and economic circumstances is endowed with a kind of tragic dignity.

Dreiser's friendship with Arthur Henry—the man to whom *Sister Carrie* was dedicated and the writer who encouraged Dreiser to begin the novel in Maumee, Ohio, in the summer of 1899—provides further insight into the relation between popular fiction and Dreiser's novels. Arthur Henry, author of *Nicholas Blood, Candidate* (1890), *A Princess* of *Arcady* (1900), and *An Island Cabin* (1902), was composing the second of three works during the same period that Dreiser composed *Sister Carrie*. *A Princess of Arcady*, the book Henry worked on while Dreiser scribbled the beginning of *Sister Carrie*, is an openly sentimentalist production, and his characters hardly come in contact with the urban world. Dreiser is supposed to have written the final chapter of Henry's book, demonstrating, if the assertion is true, his ability to provide any kind of writing needed, as he would later prove in editing the Butterick publications and providing prose that supported the conventional views of his readers. This is one more piece of evidence to suggest that Dreiser's style is a matter of conscious choice, and he could vary and control it more than some critics have suggested.

Henry devotes *A Princess of Arcady* to sentiment, and a brief discussion of the novel will show how *Sister Carrie* departs from the common run of such sentimentalism. Henry's novel follows the tale of orphans who are rescued and brought to eventual happiness as adults. In the last chapter the innocent maiden Hilda receives her first kiss from her childhood love, Pierre, after being saved from poverty and gently reared by the kindly industrialist Mr. Minot Alexander, to whom she has given the love and freshness of the daughter he never had. The pathos of childhood may be set against *Carrie*, wherein Dreiser gives us a preponderance of social rather than personal details concerning Chicago in the first few pages—and even more in the original manuscript, now restored in the Pennsylvania edition. Not so in *A Princess of Arcady*. Well into the middle of Henry's novel, Mr. Alexander looks at the toilers on his boats at dock and considers the unremitting toil of the dockworkers in almost the only socially centered passage in Henry's novel: "Whenever he looked at the world of labour and saw its poverty and narrow bounds, he felt that something was wrong; but seeing no way to remedy it, he looked away."[12] The novel immediately turns away from the matter as abruptly as Mr. Alexander has approached it. In other words, even many of Dreiser's associates were divorced from the kind of social fiction he wrote. Their descriptive details aim at the picturesque; Dreiser's show the underlying harshness of the commonplace.

Henry's last book, *An Island Cabin*, also offers us alternatives to the Dreiserian vision but has biographical interest as well, for it portrays Dreiser as an uncongenial and annoying houseguest at Henry's summer retreat. Its publication consequently ended their friendship, and Dreiser removed the dedication to Henry in the 1907 Dodge edition of *Sister Carrie*, his only change beyond altering the plagiarized passage from Ade's *Fables in Slang*. *An Island Cabin* offers insight into Dreiser's novel despite Henry's work being reportorial autobiography rather than fiction per se. Not unlike *Sister Carrie, An Island Cabin* takes as a starting point the problem of city life and the need to save five cents by walking instead of riding the streetcar. By chapter 2 Henry is philosophizing about the battle of life, the power of nature, and the interweaving of survival and kindliness as counterpoints to mundane daily activities. The philosophical framework is thus similar to *Carrie*, but with a widely different application, for the setting for Henry's musings is a small island retreat in Connecticut, which has nothing whatsoever to do with the urban world of Carrie Meeber. Henry's adventure allows what an urban experience does not—the development of his own food sources and artist's life-style. Whereas *Carrie* is the study of the potential of lower-class life, the island cabin represents Henry's bohemian-seeming but really rather middle-class escape from urban routine, as well as a set of aspirations that are the very opposite of those held by the local fishermen, whose lives Henry touches on but does not portray. Yet some locals, such as Sam, a summer caretaker, show much of the modern character that Dreiser, too, wished to capture. Henry echoes Dreiser's philosophy of language, as he says that without superficial meaningless talk, there are "multitudes who could not speak," for words are not truths,[13] but he offers no demonstration, particularly not the ponderous demonstration that is typical of Dreiser's veritism. Ellen Moers has written convincingly of how brilliantly Dreiser shows inarticulateness in Carrie and Drouet, as discussed in the chapter on style in this volume. Furthermore, Dreiser's heaping up of details that represent his fear of falling to the lowest common denominator of economic existence, which he had experienced in his childhood, distinguishes his writing from *An Island Cabin*, in which Henry offhandedly employs his ready cash and middle-class sophistication to escape economic hardship.

Not only is Henry helpful in viewing the text, of course; he was also important at several points during the composition of *Sister Carrie*. He consistently encouraged Dreiser and pressured him to finish the novel, and he arranged with his friend Anna Mallon for her typing service to type the manuscript. He also may have supplied chapter titles. Although Dreiser ultimately allowed the changes, Henry cut about 40,000 words from *Sister Carrie* so that the novel would be an acceptable length for William Heinemann, who reprinted it in Britain in his Dollar Library. Perhaps less happily, Henry also urged Dreiser to stick with his Doubleday contract whereas a cooler head might have counseled negotiating an advantageous settlement. Finally, Henry may have leaked the story of *Sister Carrie*'s suppression by Doubleday in 1902, thus bringing the novel later consideration as a "victim" of genteel prudery and a "cause" for liberal readers. Henry, in short, is deeply involved with the novel's history.

Henry's effect on the text itself was also notable. In fact, his influence is much debated and the editors of the Pennsylvania edition of *Sister Carrie* flatly declare that cuts recommended by Henry, amounting to several hundred passages, "censored, and corrupted" the novel.[14] Thirty-six thousand words were marked in block passages by Henry for cutting in roughly 200 or more instances, and Dreiser accepted most of the suggested cuts. The discussion of the restoration of the cuts by the editors of the Pennsylvania edition gives us a valuable insight into the various texts. The Pennsylvania editors find that the Drouet of the novel was made less coarsely sensual and disloyal to Carrie than the Drouet of the manuscript; Hurstwood was shown as less physically excited and his behavior became therefore more idealistic and less sexual in the revision. These two changes alone substantially alter the effect of the novel according to the editors. Other changes, the editors contend, weaken the Spencerian philosophy of the book and detract from Carrie's importance as a heroine concerned with her own morality. Dreiser, however, approved the cuts with almost no exceptions. Since the cuts may have been made in response to a recommendation not to publish the book by a reader at Harper's, the case may be argued that Dreiser under other circumstances might have retained many of the passages. How many is a moot point. In any event, along with a new ending to the book in the handwriting of Dreiser's wife, "Jug", and her stylistic suggestions, Henry's cuts and reworking of style were profound, and the Pennsylvania edition of *Sister Carrie* does, indeed, appear to be, as the editors suggest, "a new work of art, heretofore unknown," differing in characterization, philosophy, and theme (Penn, 532–35). The characters are indeed a bit more sordid in the Pennsylvania edition, and the original critics might have been that much more angry at the book; present-day readers seem to find the characters in the Pennsylvania edition more culpable and less sympathetic than the characters of the original 1900 publication. Dreiser provides less leeway for optimism, whether ironic or not. The mock-heroic, quasi-sentimental chapter titles disappear on the basis of the Pennsylvania remodeling, and the novel is lengthened by three chapters. Although the disappearance of the titles is consistent with a wish expressed by Dreiser in 1912, their disappearance darkens the mood of the book. A critic of the new edition might want the restored passages in the Pennsylvania text designated by a slightly different typeface rather than identified only in the very last pages of the textual apparatus after the editorial discussions, and even there with some emendations omitted.[15]

Many more influences on the novel might be cited. The Toledo streetcar strike, reported by Dreiser in 1894, during which scab drivers were pelted with clods of mud and chased away from damaged cars, is one notable case. Dreiser writes with a texture corresponding to his report in the strike scene depicting a similar fate for Hurstwood.[16] The sources for *Sister Carrie* suggest that the author was personally involved in the larger philosophical and literary influences of the novel's place and time. In Dreiser's case, as these background notes suggest, experience, social class, and psychology blend together into the story. It is for these reasons that the novel is a radical moral and stylistic departure from anything seen before it in the self-consciously higher order of American fiction; yet, like many other works, it is understandably the product of the life and thought of its author.

A READING

Emma Dreiser, Theodore Dreiser's sister, as a young woman
*Published by permission of Robert W. Woodruff Library, Special Collections
Department, Emory University, and Vera Dreiser*

5

The Plot

The plot of *Sister Carrie* was the book's most "immoral" feature for contemporary reviewers. The sexual fall of a beautiful woman was not an unusual item for European literature, although when French realists such as Zola and Flaubert treated fallen women in detail, the more genteel American readers often recoiled. Fallen women in American novels paid the price of sin—death, bitter and impoverished or luridly painful and ugly, rather than rising to wealth and public appeal. Americans had been fascinated with the theme since the 1790s and the publication of such novels as Susanna Rowson's *Charlotte Temple*. A few reviewers vented their spleen by complaining that "sister" Carrie was neither a nun nor much of anybody's sister, and, as mentioned previously, the typists of the original manuscript, after finishing an "iniquitous chapter" even wrote a note to Dreiser expressing readiness for more "hot and sizzling" material.[1] To Dreiser the point of the action is really to reflect society in the lives of his characters. When he refers to "evil" (192) during Hurstwood's theft, or when Mrs. Vance calls Carrie "a little sinner," Dreiser is using these concepts in a secular rather than a religious way; his focal point is not a life of sin but rather a life that is a confused and baffled longing toward higher purposes.

In Dreiser's eyes the fallen figure of his novel is Hurstwood. The destruction of Hurstwood is partly a function of his character and partly a device that provides the book's dominant action from the middle of the novel to its conclusion. Even here Dreiser is challenging a popular interest in male redemption that coincided with popular interest in woman's fall melodramas. Instead of granting his characters redemption, Dreiser expresses his sympathy and understanding for the corruption of their weak moral wills. He shows them succumbing to stronger human urges for material goods and social well-being. Hurstwood is the casualty of remorseless social and economic circumstances as binding as the forces of nature in Norris, Crane, and London, and high social standing is in no way a defense against such a fate as derives from Hurstwood's failures of character. These ideas were obvious to Dreiser, but moral critics did not welcome them as an alternative to the prevailing sense of morality in popular literature and culture. As a tragic figure, Hurstwood represents the flaws of mankind, and he is sacrificed for the general weaknesses of mankind rather than for an individualized evil.

Vice and seduction plots were not strangers to readers, certainly. *Pamela* and *Clarissa* had provided such events. Earlier in the history of the English novel, *Moll Flanders* even provides us with a prostitute-thief who is to be understood as a product of her society's desire for wealth and comfort. Thackeray's Becky Sharp in *Vanity Fair* becomes more vicious while surviving a widening range of immoral habits, although clearly in economic decline. A series of French novelists had also provided heroines of less than sterling virtue; Flaubert's Madame Bovary is perhaps the leading example of a female character far outside the bounds of American morality yet demanding the attention of American intellectuals. Balzac's *Père Goriot*, which features two daughters who abandon their father, has been cited as a possible influence on the Carrie-Hurstwood outcome. Carrie is reading this novel in the last chapter of *Sister Carrie* when Hurstwood chooses suicide. Thus, European models for Dreiser's work can be found and were being widely read in America, but the battle for sterner realism had not been so completely won by 1900 that American publishers wanted to be identified with a novel as bold as *Sister Carrie*.[2]

The Plot

In American literature, particularly popular literature, the fall of a woman—her achieving sexuality outside of marriage—was a criminal event. Hester Prynne in Nathaniel Hawthorne's *The Scarlet Letter*, published in 1850, is pilloried for such a sin. The popular literature of the newspapers of the 1870s and 1880s exposed a whole range of life, from chorus girls to crime, that did not find its way onto the library tables of America's middle-class drawing rooms. When John Hay depicted the casual kissing of a seducible young girl in his novel *The Bread-winners* in 1883, a storm of criticism was the result. But with varying degrees of success, realists began to substitute commonplace marital discord and sexual misbehavior for the metaphysical and the vulgar alike. William Dean Howells, the leader of the American realists, who brushed off Dreiser, the aspiring novelist, with the bare comment, "You know, I don't like *Sister Carrie*,"[3] managed to treat marital infidelity in *A Modern Instance*, his realistic bid to rewrite the Greek tragedy *Medea* in the American idiom. Mark Twain and Charles Dudley Warner in *The Gilded Age* offer a convincing fallen woman in Laura Hawkins, who shoots her seducer—a story line based on contemporary newspaper stories surrounding one Laura D. Fair. The authors, however, offer Laura either the punishment of living in a mental institution or the humiliation of suffering a heart attack as she attempts to lecture a hostile audience on the fate of women. None of these were promising precedents for Dreiser's depiction of a fallen woman whose material status improves.

The plot of *Sister Carrie* is relatively straightforward. Dreiser describes a pliant young girl—crude, ignorant, youthful, and unsophisticated, Dreiser says in the first two pages—who comes to Chicago to work but loses her grimy factory job owing to illness. Falling into the acquaintance of a pleasure-loving salesman, she is seduced and established in a somewhat domesticated love nest, where she begins to notice and ape the graces of higher social classes. The heroine gains in grace and even triumphs in a local theatrical production that mirrors her experience and draws out her emotional brilliance. Mesmerized by her youth and freshness, a second lover—an established family man and saloon manager—seduces her away from the first seducer, and, absconding with money purloined from the safe of his confiding employers, takes her to Canada and New York. Owing to the mischance of pursuit and detection, the second lover returns the money and the pair encounter the difficulties of establishing themselves in a new environment without sufficient financial resources. Finally, the heroine, now schooled in the arts of the world, succeeds on the stage and abandons her decaying lover, who is overcome by the struggle for life and commits suicide. He is buried in a potter's field as the former shopgirl rises to ever greater heights of worldly success—but a success that does not satisfy her inner longings and loneliness.

To bare the plot in this way as a sexualized sentimental melodrama is by no means to demean it. In fact, this sort of bald recounting may suggest how much Dreiser's style and philosophical intrusions, discussed elsewhere, added to its interest. Most significant to contemporaries was that Carrie is a morally weak young woman—although Dreiser provides the reader with sociological commentary that is an apologia—who is overcome by the desire for material objects. Material and emotional concerns sway her into sexual liaisons that were unacceptable to many conventional readers, yet she successfully gains her goals in the material world without a hint of punishment. The author purposefully maintains her emotional sadness, but whereas she earlier stared from a tenement door at clerks, by the end of the novel she looks out the window of the finest hotel in New York to see a male pedestrian fall on the ice. Many critics and even the firm that published the book viewed this representation of ascendancy as immoral, yet if we look at the novel as a critique of the minds of the characters, Dreiser is highly critical of their mental power and integrity. Carrie's emotional yearning has a materialistic component; Drouet is a venal pleasure seeker; Hurstwood a selfish egotist.

The real story of Dreiser's Sister Emma and L. A. Hopkins is the immediate basis of what appears to be the central event in the plot. Hopkins was a clerk at the main Chicago saloon of Chapin & Gore until he ran off with $3,500 from the safe and with Sister Emma accompanying him. The pair fled to New York, leaving behind Hopkins's wife and 18-year-old daughter. As the newspapers reported on the unfolding drama, the problem of marital infidelity and divorce was raised, and, finally, Hopkins returned the money to escape prosecution.[4] Emma was fully qualified for the role of the mysterious other woman in this case, as the extant photograph reveals her to be roundly plump, small-waisted, and full-featured, a reasonably attractive candidate for success on the stage. By the time Dreiser saw her in New York, however, her liaison with Hopkins had deteriorated, as had her looks and her life. The rise of Carrie was an altogether different fiction grafted on to this one notorious incident. Emma did indeed leave Hopkins, but she did so by Theodore and his brother Paul rescuing her from abject poverty and self-pity.

Lesser components of Carrie's story were also available to Dreiser through his reading. The approach of a masher toward a likely girl on the train into Chicago had been so well represented by George Ade in "The Fable of the Two Mandolin Player and the Willing Performer," in *Fables in Slang*, that Dreiser simply picked up Ade's material and copied it into the opening pages of the novel to characterize the "masher" type in Drouet. Propriety called for introductions through intermediaries who could vouch for both parties. Thus the characterization on which the first eleven chapters stand is derived from a technique of meeting women "improperly" that was already current in humorous literature. Here, as with other instances, Dreiser adopts the impropriety as part of the character's nature and thus builds impropriety into the premise on which the plot event is based. Drouet, and later Hurstwood, populate a self-interested social world, a model far different from that demanded in fiction by later nineteenth-century moralists. Yet, his portrayal makes good sense for the world of train and omnibus riders, public school goers, and others thrown into a wide array of circumstances because they were not of the upper-middle and upper classes. Typically, the "realism" of *Sister Carrie* is of just this sort. Dreiser has turned to lower and less competitive economic classes in an urban environment, but he has presented life in high rather than low literature.

Dreiser takes pains to suggest that Carrie has poor alternatives or none in her life, and this is a central feature in her motivation. Carrie must first seek employment in department stores and factories, and she has negative experiences: men cast lustful eyes on her and make veiled propositions; wages are inadequate; female companionship is low and coarse, even when other factory girls are kindly intentioned. Despair seems a natural outcome. In this, Dreiser the pessimist is actually following lines that had been laid down as social assumptions since immediately following the Civil War. Reverend T. De Witt Talmage in *The Abominations of Modern Society* had praised the woman who could overcome a drunken husband, children, and "The Massacre of Needle and Sewing Machine" to appear properly dressed in church on the Sabbath.[5] He noted the viciousness of employers who held down women's wages in the sweatshops. An optimist, he declared that unskilled labor would always be poorly paid, but competent skilled labor would "eventually" make its own standard; and parents who sent their daughters unskilled into the world were no better than assassins. Carrie fits Talmage's mold: "To thousands of young women of New York to-day there is only this alternative: starvation or dishonor. Many of the largest mercantile establishments of our cities are accessory to these abominations; and from their large establishments there are scores of souls being pitched off into death; *and their employers know it!*" (Talmage, 104). One of the notable variations between the novel in 1900 and the Pennsylvania edition is that a number of passages in which repulsive characters blatantly proposition Carrie were deleted in 1900 and are restored to the Pennsylvania edition, which depicts a world even more directly in line with Talmage's complaint. That critics hated this aspect of the book even in its softened form is telling evidence of the strength of established social and economic forces working against reform, and the unwillingness of contemporary Americans to confront the sexual and personal problems inherent in labor conditions. Thus Dreiser's alternative to suffering—Carrie's moving in with Drouet—was a radical alternative.

The home, however, is not a solid influence to a middle-class American just removed from immigrant status. Dreiser takes considerable pains to point out the saving nature of "excellent home principles" (60), which are absent from Carrie's life. In her family life, as manifest at the Hanson's flat, no affection supplies a rescuing force. In substitution for humanity, Dreiser gives us the most exaggerated bathos of the sullen Hanson and the downtrodden Minnie. Dreiser plays conventional morality, popular melodrama, and pragmatic motivation against each other repeatedly: following Carrie's vague twitch of habit concerning a homecoming hour at the Hansons', Dreiser brilliantly takes us with no transition from the prosaic date of a masher and his girl to Minnie's overwrought nightmare with its dreadful images of falling and drowning (61) and then on to a casual social conversation between men of the world—Drouet's casual invitation to his manager-friend Hurstwood, for the first time, to "come out some evening," which is the mundane beginning of the end for all (62). Hurstwood's home life will later expand this way of managing theme.

Dreiser was not strictly alone in focusing on social propositions. Even Joaquin Miller, the author of California gold-rush stories, famous for parading down London streets in chaps and cowboy boots, described the ugly underside of urban society in a grim urban melodrama titled *The Destruction of Gotham*, published in 1886. Miller, like Dreiser, sends a farmgirl to the city without friends or a job. Miller's unnamed country girl is pursued by a vicious crone who kidnaps her, arranges for her defilement by a wealthy villain, and leaves her crazed and starving with her child. The evils of the city bear the desperate woman inexorably to her grave, starve her small child, and fail to bring retribution to the rich seducer. Miller, although approaching Dreiser's themes, offers us a saintly reporter and some pious hopes for the influence of God on man the animal. The piety is hardly justified by the plot, which climaxes in the apocalyptic rise of the poor in revolt against the city's rich. Miller's exploration of urban social problems parallels Dreiser's: vice surrounds a poor but pretty woman and very likely will overwhelm her if her personality is not strongly anchored. However, whereas Miller's plot follows an inevitable downward course; Dreiser's transfers the downward course from Carrie to Hurstwood, and Dreiser's novel seems to chronicle the economic "rise" of Carrie. However, Dreiser retains the same overall movement of the novel; he transfers the victimization to Hurstwood, a transfer that gave many reviewers the feeling that the novel follows Hurstwood and leaves Sister Carrie. The parallelism of plots really shows us that the novel is about a "situation." The emotional development of the works is markedly similar, even down to the strikes at the end of the action and the climax surrounding the deaths of the chief figures of interest.

Sequences from the play within the novel, Carrie's first amateur theatrical—*Under the Gaslight*, which leads to Carrie's first triumph in her quest for the better things in life—also echo the plot of the novel. The heroine of the drama is an outcast like Carrie, so the part calls on Carrie for special responsiveness. Hurstwood, the affluent and well-connected manager who draws on his colleagues with the power of a "Roman" senator to support the activity, is at the apex of his magnetism in a world akin to that described in the play. Drouet is little better than the male figures in the drama. At a crucial moment when the acting is going badly, he appears backstage and supplies Carrie with new warmth and courage, but his "enthusiasm was due to the mere spirit of the occasion," like all his other thoughts, superficial rather than sincere (134). Carrie, swayed by the likeness of her role to her predicament, reenters in the next act and without even speaking projects "The magic of passion, which will yet dissolve the world" (135). For the first time we see the "emotional greatness" that Dreiser sees in her. Carrie symbolizes her own quest, for when she is acting on the stage, removed from her two lovers, and seemingly unattainable—distanced by the footlights—both men are driven into new frenzies of desire for her. That which is beautiful, bright, and distant is what most stirs the soul. So Hurstwood desires Carrie's freshness, so Carrie desires the beautiful lights and amusements of the splendid restaurants, so Drouet in a lesser and therefore less potentially tragic manner responds to Carrie even at the moment when the two are severing their relationship because of Drouet's jealousy over Hurstwood and Carrie's quest for a higher level of appreciation and refinement. The climactic moment is the statement in the play, "society is a terrible avenger of insult," comparable to Siberian wolves (134). Carrie and Laura, the heroine of the play, merge spiritually, and by the next page of the novel, she "had done something which was above his [Hurstwood's] sphere" spiritually. The adjusted reality Dreiser will offer is two very brief personal shows of independent spirit when Carrie speaks after the play. Hurstwood becomes the aggressor in the novel at this point, Carrie having established a personality of sorts. His is the position in society that will most fit the play's dictum.

Carrie's longing is most potent as a nearly passive yearning in the larger movements of circumstance. The masculine immediacy of Hurstwood's desire is the foil of the real Carrie and the artificial Laura. Carrie's very slight responses are important, more important than we give them credit for being in some cases, for she must not be seen as being in control of her destiny, a note false to Dreiser's concept of the world. The role gives her an artificial power, but with real consequences. It externalizes the melodrama of her vulnerability better than she can live or express it through her own limited resources. The sentimental melodrama is her reality. Hurstwood, on the other hand, by his position and the assumptions accompanying it, represents a stronger force capable of battling larger forces—the Greeks would have called those forces destiny or fate—more frontally, and Dreiser soon begins to label Hurstwood as tragic by noting that the play created in him "the tragedy of affection" (138), leading later to "an elation which was tragic in itself" (148). His force is so great that he deludes Carrie into almost believing herself in love with him (149). Dreiser thus ensures that we will recognize that Hurstwood will suffer a tragic defeat by succumbing after his own fall to the social forces that would condemn Carrie and Laura. To this extent, the focus of the novel does shift from Carrie to Hurstwood in plotting the tragedy.

Like Carrie's social situation as reflected in *Under the Gaslight*, Hurstwood's standing may be viewed in terms of contemporary documents, but in his case the documents that offer comparisons are external to the novel and must be brought into the discussion only as relevant cultural artifacts. The theft of his employer's money by Hurstwood may be viewed in terms of the fall and redemption of thieves as a popular nineteenth-century topic. Will Carleton's bathetic popular poem "Over the Hill to the Poorhouse" of 1871, which featured a mother sent to the poorhouse because her social-climbing children did not want her around the house, was answered by "Over the Hill from the Poorhouse" a year later in which her reformed horse thief son, having been a convict and gone West to make his fortune, returns to establish her and himself by a cozy fireside. Thievery is placed more in the category of "wild oats" than of evil, and the humanizing humility of sin and repentance prove more virtuous than accepted and conventional, but rigid and sanctimonious, sustained social propriety. *Hill's Manual of Social and Business Forms* takes a similar position on forgiveness in a section on that subject and reprinted "Over the Hill to the Poorhouse" facing its counterpart "From" on a facing page (Hill, 468–69). Indeed, *Hill's Manual* also reprinted Whittier's "Maud Muller" where a poor girl does not wed a judge and rise in state, while harmoniously naturalizing him; with its lament for "what might have been" the poem advocates seizing the chance, although perhaps not in the way that Sister Carrie and Hurstwood did. Certainly it would not suggest the premeditated crime of L. A. Hopkins and Sister Emma in the real event lying behind the plot; although, as noted before, the newspaper stories of the time suggested that Hopkins would attempt to rejoin his employer, repenting his miscue.[6]

Dreiser stalled in the writing of the novel at the point where Hurstwood seizes the chance of taking $10,000 from the unluckily unlocked safe of Fitzgerald and Moy. Dreiser apparently found it difficult to account for the theft because he was not comfortable with the mood of Hurstwood. Specifically, he felt that he could make Hurstwood neither drunk and therefore guiltless of criminality nor coldly sober and therefore fully resolved and in control of himself. Dreiser depicts Hurstwood trembling between desire for Carrie and duty to his employer, a reduplication of the problem of flesh and spirit that Carrie felt in taking Drouet's financial support, but now condensed into a single moment and magnified from $20 to a much higher figure. From Dreiser's revelation to that of biographer Robert Elias that maintaining the moral ambiguity of the theft was a stumbling block, all critics have accepted the emphasis on "the predicament of the individual whose mind is less strongly constituted" (192). The true nature of Dreiser's genius in writing about common people rather than heroic figures masquerading in common garb is never more apparent than here. "Instinct" and a "wavering mind" hold Hurstwood in thrall while the safe door swings shut and seals his doom, making final the theft that he knows is a scandal and a mistake from the very first moment. Nor has Dreiser avoided the moral problem, for he identifies Hurstwood's amorality clearly: "The true ethics of the situation [ethics which would have saved him, of course] never once occurred to him, and never would have, under any circumstances" (193). The personal weakness of his central characters is in fact the center of Dreiser's interest, the very universal puzzle he wishes to present to us. In this, Hurstwood corresponds to Carrie. Obviously, the manager could have kept the money over the weekend with a stern reprimand to his cashier on Monday morning. Such decisiveness, however, would not have been like Hurstwood, nor would it have aligned Hurstwood with Carrie for the readers.

Despite Dreiser's uncertainty in plotting the event, such stories as Hurstwood's existed prominently in popular literature, but often with "reform" endings. *John Smith's Funny Adventures on a Crutch* by A. F. Hill recounts Hill's visit to St. Louis and his meeting with Albert Hague. Hague, like Hurstwood, "much to the astonishment and amazement of all who knew him, . . . stole ten thousand dollars from his employer, and absconded."[7] Hague escaped to California after falling to temptation "in an evil moment" but restored the money owing to ill conscience three weeks later and was embarked on a new life as a salesman in a wholesale house in St. Louis when Hill met him. Hill concludes that he will not tell the new employers: "The strictly 'pious,' with the blindness that too often characterizes them, may censure me for not warning his employers, but let them do so. Do they think, that when a man commits one crime, he is necessarily lost, forever?" (A. F. Hill, 239). However, it is suggestive of the prevailing attitudes that Hill goes on to reason his position for another two paragraphs: "Frown on vice as much as you please; but do not frown on all who once yield to temptation" (A. F. Hill, 239). In fact, Dreiser's portrayal may be the more realistic one in depicting Hurstwood as wishing to go back but knowing the impossibility except as a fantasy. Attesting to the popularity of the story of a man's vice reformed is another almost identical story in *Knots Untied: Or, Ways and By-Ways in the Hidden Life of American Detectives* by Officer George S. McWatters, late of the Metropolitan Police of New York, recounting the story of "young Worden" under the title "Lottery Ticket, No. 1710."[8] Worden robbed a safe that seemed to have been left inadvertently unlocked while the owner slept, but he was captured by the detective in another city when he tried to cash in an accompanying lottery ticket. Worden, too, offered to repay the money, reformed, and "is now a prominent and wealthy man of Chicago," having succeeded in business in New York (McWatters, 150). So the genre goes, with story after story of temptation and reform. As with the material from the industrial romances and popular fiction by Bertha Clay, a crucial point to remember is that Dreiser's novel presented itself as a higher order of fiction, not as cheap popular fiction. *Sister Carrie* was to be published not as a cheap-paper romance but rather in hard cover by a major publishing firm catering to an educated audience and seeking serious critical reviews. As such, these themes from vulgar experience were brought into a cultural context where they were new.

It can fairly be said that *Sister Carrie* is one of the most pessimistic masterpieces in American literature. In large part this is because Dreiser cuts off the possibility of reform for any of the characters. Hurstwood, chief representative of the human desire to gain pleasure, "to make a try for Paradise, whatever might be the result" (151), as Dreiser phrases his thinking with ominous foreshadowing in chapter 22, goes spiralling downward in the story rather rapidly, although at one point we are told that the decline takes place over three years or more. The implacable, incontrovertible downward course of Hurstwood to the novel's end is powerful and compelling, but remorseless, offering no chance for reconciliation. Exterior events seem to punish Hurstwood with cold and misery as much as the economic events of a truculent and unresponsive partner in a cheap business investment punish his will to succeed economically. In each area of the plot, Hurstwood finds defeat, and Carrie finds further reasons for distancing herself from him. Unpleasant social experiences are wed to a depressive social determinism, an oppressively sterner realism. Hurstwood's Sisyphusian grandeur lies in his stolid battle against the multiplex forces bearing him downward; readers cannot help but identify with his pride in the face of adversity. The plot is even more formidable because it turns to extremely localized experience instead of heroic events. The novel plays out the decline of the central male figure in nickels and dimes. Domesticity becomes as much symbolic as it is oriented to events. Where the dynamism of figures in Dreiser's later novels could be viewed in terms of their sexual or economic history—the extensive detailing of Frank Cowperwood's streetcar financing in Philadelphia in *The Financier* being the most obvious example—*Sister Carrie* gives us the details of a New York City flat, a Chicago boardinghouse, or the Hurstwood versus the Hanson family. In each case, details are built around the financing of the family life at the level of buying dinner or an evening newspaper. At no time do we get an optimistic sense of dimensions of pleasure outside the house, where partners are usually separate. Hurstwood later in decline gambles and loses or cheats the grocer and the Italian paper seller. Dreiser shows Hurstwood gambling outside the apartment in order to show him falling into vice through the desperation of a shallow man driven to extremes. His careful return of correct change to the kitchen table after buying groceries is equally weighty in expressing a kind of humility in his pride (285). This detailing of domestic survival is important for it leads naturally to the detailing of Hurstwood's survival outside the home later in the novel. The gradual downward progression from internal domestic security to the homelessness of the work-seeker, scab—and, by progressive stages to vagrant, pan-handler, bum, and outcast derelict—derives much of its power by replacing the previous details of morning breakfast at the Hurstwood home with Carrie and Hurstwood adjusting to New York in downward progressions. Shortly after losing $60 in poker, Hurstwood abandons his good clothes and pride and in an argument confronts Carrie with their false marriage—an ultimate family crisis that soon propels Carrie into her new life. Hurstwood takes over the role Carrie had held at the Hansons, reckoning against her paltry weekly wages, and her feeling of despair. Carrie, taken by the Vances to Sherry's in New York, takes over Hurstwood's environment of glittering glass and white napery, the world he can only haunt as a ghostly lobby-sitter avoiding acquaintances from his previous life. The plot brings both characters to reversals of situation that provide mirror images of the other. Hence, Carrie's sadness is all the more poignant to the reader because of the feeling of *déjà vu*—we were there before. But now it is Hurstwood falling to destruction—the very events that Minnie's dream foretold for Carrie. Dreiser's switching of roles unifies the plot, for it explains to us the power of the novel to be depressing and great at the same time. Hurstwood is bitterly repaid for not seeing the beggar when he was a rich man.

The fall of Hurstwood deserves special attention, of course, because it is undoubtedly the area where Dreiser embodies his own deepest fears of death and dissolution in the face of economic noncompetitiveness. Hurstwood represents established but tenuous wealth. Hurstwood's family life, as well, places him within a circle of large Chicago homes and expansive starched white shirtfronts prominently represented in the era's newspaper social pages. As noted, Hurstwood is imagined in the novel well above the likely real standing of such a person, and even further above his real life model, Emma's lover Hopkins. Hurstwood's real purpose in the plot, and the tragic intensity that causes him to seem to take over the plot, is that he is the ultimate social victim of economic and social prejudice. Carrie was never enough of an Emma Bovary to justify an end such as the French heroine's, but Hurstwood is endowed with higher potential, partly because Dreiser identifies with him as a male one might hazard a guess, but he still fulfills Dreiser's need to show how the world damages its Carries, in the generic sense of Carrie as everyone's vulnerable emotional self. At the same time, Hurstwood as an invention allowed Dreiser to write a novel that was above the run of a seduction tragedy such as Miller's *Destruction of Gotham*.

Prior to his adventures with Carrie, however, Hurstwood's family, whom he will desert, provides background for his tragedy in two places in the plot. First, they represent social propriety in the world of Chicago and New York—the great naturalist force surrounding Dreiser's characters as certainly as the Alaskan wilderness surrounds

White Fang in Jack London's novel; the melodramatized social force surrounding Laura in *Under the Gaslight* is explicitly identified in terms of a wolf-pack. Such representative depictions of propriety bulked larger in the later novels, such as *Jennie Gerhardt* and *The Financier*. First, the family represents a block on Hurstwood's natural urges and excitement and then a reprise of his fall in their late momentary reappearance to take a boat trip to Europe just before Hurstwood's body takes its last boat ride to Potter's Field. The transparent device of having Hurstwood give his wife title to their house and control of much of his solid property completes the economic vice in which the fallen manager finds himself trapped. Such an economic arrangement seems at least as plausible as Huck and Jim fleeing south on the Mississippi to escape slavery, but not much more so. This plotting deprives Hurstwood of room for maneuvering, which would have made his tragedy less inevitable. The inevitability must come forth strongly and inescapably.

Reports to Mrs. Hurstwood of George's doings provide detail by detail a trail that brings her to confront him, in bitterness and jealousy over her fading appeal, about the very theatrical event that had inflamed his desire for Carrie. Their most significant confrontation, in fact, comes as Julia arranges her hair in front of a mirror, appropriate for the contrasting action of Carrie's youth and freshness supplanting her mature calculating demeanor. This contrasting scene follows Hurstwood's mistaken recognition of a peculiarly happy domesticity in the picture of homelife and fireside presented to him after his day's work. Drouet and Carrie will play out a similarly awkward confrontation in their flat, also punctuated by materialistic concerns. Of a lower status and less powerful than the Hurstwoods', Drouet's and Carrie's argument is appropriately more muddled and less sharply defined in its issues. But Carrie's plight is more fully dramatized, perhaps to the point of bathos, because Carrie's alternative is literally "the street, without a place to lay her head" (168), but Hurstwood, too, catches a glimmer of financial implication "shining" in his wife's glance (160) and is finally left standing on the street.

Hurstwood's theft of money from the safe of Fitzgerald and Moy is merely a symbolic moment that encapsulates a general worldview and punctuates his deteriorating situation with a climactic impulse. The ultimate causative force connecting the events of the plot is that all the resources of moral strength—personal fiber, homelife—are irrelevant to the weak and needy, the yearning. Deprivation breeds vulnerability; Dreiser senses that the conventional morality of his day is lacking a fundamental factor: it deals falsely with the motivation of real need and emotional need alike. With the safe accidentally closing, Dreiser preserves the sense of external force bearing on weak wills, which helps the reader accept Hurstwood's movement into Carrie's outcast standing in the world. Thus Dreiser's naturalism is more sophisticated than that of some other writers because it is integrated so fully within the personalities of his characters before emerging as "plot." Endowing Hurstwood's wife with the power of a "pythoness" is merely further indication of how close Dreiser was to thinking in overtly naturalistic animal images; yet from that kind of writing he held back. The novel has some similarity to the style of Frank Norris, its earliest booster at Doubleday, in the family scenes indicated here, both early and late, but moving the guilt from Hurstwood as cynic to Hurstwood as victim of a weak will blown about by the winds of sexual urgency places him in a more human than animal situation, far more appealing than Henry Fleming in Crane's *Red Badge of Courage*, for example.

The details of decline in New York City are similarly useful in defining the world in which all characters move. Hurstwood in the grip of economic necessity becomes subject to biological forces, and he takes over Carrie's rocking chair and finds even further solace in the newspaper—thus recapturing a kind of cut-off indifference that reechoes Carrie's evenings at the Hansons' flat, which limited her original entry into urban life. He comes to convey the dismal gloom, dullness, and brooding apathy that Dreiser describes in him in chapter 39. Thus, Carrie must attempt the stage out of the same necessity that drove her to Drouet: "She was not going to be dragged into poverty and something worse to suit him" (272). The confused strands of the actual morality of the situation are hardly relevant. The flat becomes "a load to bear" (295) to Carrie. Thus, the plot retrieves and reechoes early unpalatable experiences, helping us to understand Carrie's dissatisfaction. The Hanson experience is reechoed in the plot as a component of Hurstwood's deterioration.

Later in the plot Carrie, in distinction to Hurstwood, achieves a spiritual vacuum in conjunction with her economic rise. She learns from Hurstwood that their marriage is not binding. The language is that of melodrama, but the action is thoroughly domestic. "A thunderbolt in camp" is how Dreiser describes Carrie's suggestion that Hurstwood get a job. Carrie's "dawning independence" gives her courage to observe (282). Observing, she recognizes her ability to do better than those around her. Her ability to earn a place and then to rise in it, in fact, is part of the crucial exchange of roles that really reflects Dreiser's naturalist philosophy at its most subtle. For the exchange of youthful appeal, by chance, as the breadwinning feature, for worldly grace and suavity is merely a changing of the guard. The sentimental imagery accreted around "little soldiers" (beginning on 287) as the Broadway starlets and the "walled city" as the world that they inhabit is Dreiser's way of representing the rigidity of social force and its external glitter and splendor to the outsider. Such elevated language escapes into the stilted oratory of the moral textbooks and censors of the later nineteenth century, leaving Dreiser's character behind in the naturalistic world. Sandy Petrey contends that "conventional feelings proclaim their own falseness, and society presents no other kind."[9] Such passages are not ironic in intent; they are intended to show other levels of mental and emotional pain—"agony" is too strong a word— available to the yearning protagonists. The language of sentiment, in other words, is real to the characters in the plot and is part of the world's limitation in interpreting them. The chance nature of Carrie's rise, however, is clearly laid to her comparative youth.

Hurstwood is impelled to make some kind of major attempt to overcome his and Carrie's decline, particularly as Dreiser shows Carrie advancing and separating from him through her own success, which she even begins to hide from him in chapter 39, as her pay increases from $12 to $18 a week. The streetcar strike places Hurstwood within a violence that externalizes the tragedy of his decline and provides the full panoply of Dreiser's plot effects, including the battle scenes of the Brooklyn street. This episode provides a context of violence that has a social impact. Even the winter setting adds the antihuman power of coldness typical of Jack London's Arctic novels and consistent with the movement from warmth and security to cold and need that dominates the novel (see Moers 1969, 149–51). Hurstwood is beaten, cursed, cut and bleeding, and grazed by a gunshot before lurching off into a blizzard, his streetcar blocked a mile from the car barns. He battles the pain of freezing weather, poor food, filthy surroundings, all at a time when Carrie is gaining in appreciation, light, and warmth. His responses show not weakness, as some phrases hint in the text and others deny, but rather notable strength. The force of Hurstwood's will is by no means impugned, even when he comments "weakly" (313) and his gunshot wound is a "mere scratch" (313). Hurstwood has shown already that he "was no coward in spirit," responding with "a solid determination to stick it out" (310). Hurstwood, in the end, is defeated by forces larger than he could reasonably be expected to overcome, and his bare comment on the case, "That's a pretty tough game over there" (313), shows him to be humbly understated in a crushing personal defeat. Thus, plot and action blend to develop in Hurstwood the true tragic resignation. The fatalism of tragic heroism reverberates in the restricted expression.

Chapters from 42 to 45 seem so inexorable that they add significantly to the depressing mood of the novel. The section climaxes with the lengthy description of a strange captain who lines up derelicts, among them Hurstwood, solicits money for lodgings—the men are no longer even competent to beg for themselves—and places the men in flophouses each night. This final lowering of fortune brings Hurstwood to the brink of suicide, but the sequence of chapters on his decline begins after his major defeat by the strikers' violence in Brooklyn. By counterpoint, the same three chapters include Carrie's first venturing a line from the chorus of her Broadway show, followed by her meteoric rise to stardom and her accompanying abandonment of Hurstwood. Here, in Hurstwood's moment of total defeat, his greatness impresses itself on the reader, perhaps in spite of Dreiser's reservations, for

Hurstwood, like Milton's Satan in *Paradise Lost*, may have partly escaped his creator's intention in his battle against overawing circumstances.

Chapter 42 is so profoundly tragic that it encapsulates the entire cycle of the novel, particularly as it concerns Hurstwood. As with Hurstwood's taking the money from Fitzgerald and Moy's, Carrie's leaving Hurstwood is not fully a matter of decision. Lola has offered Carrie a cheaper more agreeable apartment we are told and has been rejected, but when Carrie moves upward in the Broadway show, she requires new clothes, so she takes a room with Lola to save money. Thus, economic need drives Carrie, but the drive is coupled with a misjudgment of Hurstwood that is as notable as his and Drouet's earlier misjudgments of her: "Those who look upon Hurstwood's Brooklyn venture as an error of judgment will none the less realize the negative influence on him of the fact that he had tried and failed. Carrie got a wrong idea of it. He said so little that she imagined he had encountered nothing worse than the ordinary roughness—quitting so soon in the face of this seemed trifling. He did not want to work" (313–14). Even the shape of the sentences sounds like Hurstwood's voice. As Hurstwood declines into muddled delusions, Carrie finds herself "strong in capability": "The reliance of others made her feel as if she must, and when she must she dared" (315). Dreiser writes with the simplicity of a primer at this point. Carrie sees Hurstwood "drooping," and sensing "something cruel somewhere" (319) and unable to figure it out she actually regrets betraying Drouet. She manifests her regret by borrowing $20—the exact sum with which Drouet had begun his seduction of her, to leave Hurstwood. As in the earlier case, the money she leaves in her goodbye note to Hurstwood is green and soft. Thus, the plot has come full circle, with Carrie exiting her relationship with the male remnant of Chicago life much as she had entered that life. Hurstwood, for his part, wanders burgeoning areas of New York on the day of her desertion much as the heroine had first entered Chicago. The central elements of the plot are restated; the economics reechoed; the personal desperation transferred to the drooping ex-manager by the rising professional theatrical trouper.

In chapter 43, some of Dreiser's finest writing establishes the nature of Carrie's success, heavily stressing its chance nature. Carrie's picture appears in the paper not because of her ability but because of the sociology of the times. Yet she rapidly discovers a new generalized economic truth of her new social status—that "a little money brought her nothing" (324). Carrie's photo graces Broadway advertising, but the "halcyon intention" of one show's manager is to cut her out of the show after the first week, telling the author not to kick because the part is so weak. She is thus treated by others as an object rather than a person. When she succeeds for sexual reasons—"It was the kind of frown they would have loved to force away with kisses. All the gentlemen yearned toward her" (326)—it is the leading actor who kicks and is put off, in turn. Emphasizing the nature of Carrie's "triumph," a newspaper review cites the "characteristic perversity" of audiences to explain why she has been singled out. While larger social forces buffet Hurstwood downward, comparable social chances and perversities buffet Carrie upward. The reviewer concludes in Dreiserian tone, "The vagaries of fortune are indeed curious" (327). In counterpoint to Carrie, Hurstwood is found at the end of chapter 43 in a dingy, motheaten hotel lobby, reading in the dramatic items of his newspaper Carrie's admission to the lights, ornaments, carriages, flowers, and warmth of the "walled city." Dreiser endows him with the "grim resolution of a bent, bedraggled, but unbroken pride" (328), pushing him one step closer to his ultimate role as tragic hero and victim of the social world he inhabits.

Chapter 44 moves Carrie to a sumptuous hotel. The hotel's need for publicity and glamour reduces the cost of her elegant salon below the cost of her last flat with Hurstwood, the sum of $3 a week. Now Carrie is brought to "see" that her "name is worth something" (329). This broader social lesson is softened, however, by the reassertion of her one friendly connection. Mrs. Vance rediscovers Carrie, affectionately calling her a "little sinner" not because Carrie sins, but as a mischievous designation reflecting Carrie's unexpected rise to stardom. Carrie now discovers that she has surpassed the Vances and is left feeling "as if she were the one to condescend" (332). Dreiser, however, uses the moment to bring back echoes of the opening of the novel, as Carrie receives "*mash notes*": "Only she was sufficiently wise to distinguish between her old condition and her new one. . . . She smiled to think that men should suddenly find her so much more attractive" (333). The reintroduction of her last suitor Ames is prepared by the reentry of Mrs. Vance, of course, and he will be reintroduced only to the successful version of Carrie. But is her attractiveness "sudden," in fact, or is it the result of a fairly long apprenticeship, marked at each stage by the next higher level of male finding her attractive, from shop clerks and Drouet up the scale? The feeling of suddenness lies in the level achieved, not in the woman who achieves it. Simultaneously, Hurstwood in his cheap hotel falls more deeply into the habit of thinking of old days, literally saving and counting "until his health was affected," Dreiser tells us (337). Installed in the Broadway Central as a choreboy, he sickens, emerges from a hospital shrunk to 135 pounds, and becomes a complete outcast. All is complete except his final descent into despair and suicide with the words "What's the use?"

The reversal of the social fortunes of the two central characters is a paradigm of the reversal in status of the tragic hero. Hurstwood in declining circumstances is capable of a sort of nobility toward Carrie and stolidity towards his own fate that is the fitting recompense for his tragic flaw—the hubristic youthful passion that he permitted to shear away his prized circumspection. Dreiser's insistence on chance and sociological and historical circumstance is less a judgment on the nature of her character than on the world's inability to fulfill the generalized longing for better things. Walter Benn Michaels has aptly linked this feeling not to moral punishment of Carrie but rather to Dreiser's sense of the effect of money in a capitalist society, and our sense of later heroes like Clyde Griffiths in *An American Tragedy* bears out this thinking.[10] Carrie will never be satisfied, and the holding out of Ames as a higher step on the ladder does little really to suggest a solution for Carrie. The concluding chapter 47, written after the manuscript version to bring it into balance, enlarges on these themes with fulsome sentiment, but the fact remains that such outlines of human desire and the relationship of social dictate and prejudice to personal circumstance are consistent with everything that has gone before. Yet, the tragic power of the novel comes from our sense that Hurstwood pays too much for the indiscretion he has committed. All the parties were self-interested, after all, and thus Hurstwood is not a unique transgressor. The social environment influenced each character equally. In some sense, Hurstwood's early love of Carrie is treated with some hint of hopefulness compounded by self-delusion. His punishment for his fall, however, is total, remorseless, irreversible, and awful.

6

Style

Dreiser's style has been a controversial aspect of his work from the beginning. He has been accused of being awkward in sentence structure, inept and occasionally flatly wrong in word selection and meaning, and mixed and disorganized in voice and tone. Yet several scholars have found a great deal of interest in the variations of style and tone in *Sister Carrie* and have suggested that the style of the novel was well calculated to achieve the thematic ends Dreiser sought. A holistic reading of the novel calls on us to regard everything in the novel as contributing to the reader's feelings and responses. We may take the viewpoint that Dreiser attempted to show limited intellects propelled by vague feelings and desires—not to *tell* in elevated language but to reflect in limited voice the very limitations that interested him. With the exception of words literally wrong in context, Dreiser's so-called inept style is as important interpretively as smooth style and perhaps has an even greater influence on the reader's responses. Awkward style, in fact, corresponds to the awkwardly mixed social experience portrayed.

Models of language were plentiful, of course, and one formative influence, after allowing for Dreiser's early reading of books such as

Hill's Manual, was his work as a newspaper writer. Unlike the stripped simplicity that seems to shape modern Hemingwayesque prose, language in the newspaper pieces collected in such useful primary sources as *Theodore Dreiser Journalism. Volume One, Newspaper Writings, 1892–1895*, varied widely from the simple to the melodramatic. Articles are racier than present-day newspaper readers would anticipate. Dreiser's descriptions of the transit strike in 1894 for the Toledo *Blade* fit as easily in the novel as in the newspaper.[1] Much the same can be said of the articles reprinted in *Selected Magazine Articles of Theodore Dreiser*.[2] "The Curious Shifts of the Poor," originally printed in *Demorest's Family Magazine*, has been recognized as the basis of chapters 45 and 47 of *Sister Carrie* describing Hurstwood's situation as an outcast needing a flophouse bed.

Before he became a journalist, Dreiser experienced other important styles of writing and thinking. Richard Lingeman notes that the young Dreiser devoured *Hill's Manual of Social and Business Forms* around 1878 (Lingeman, 45). Not only does the manual contain such sentimental gems as Will Carleton's "Over the Hill to the Poorhouse"—with its picture of well-to-do family members rejecting crusty old ma—and Whittier's "Maud Muller," depicting a farmgirl who weds a judge; it also includes material that duplicates these themes in the conventional rhetoric of the period, with its pretense of social form. *Hill's Manual* establishes absolutes in the pompous language that marks some of the philosophical discourses in *Sister Carrie*. A passage on toleration for the fallen has already been cited, but the moralizing was pervasive. A randomly selected sentence on penmanship reads, "The person who may apply for a situation as teacher, clerk, or any position where intellectual ability is required, finds a beautifully written letter the best recommendation that can be sent when applying for that position" (Hill, 40). The rules, the style in which they are written, the atmosphere of judgment, are all typical of the world that envelops Dreiser's characters and from which he wishes to differentiate their own malleable and sensual weaknesses. *Hill's Manual* is one of many such models on which Dreiser could have built his prose, whether he presented the style directly or with a certain detachment bordering on irony.

The alternative to the formal style and locutions of the conventional essayists was the language of the newcomer, the poor outsiders seeking the benefits of urban culture—the lowly. Many reviewers objected to the coarseness of the language in the novel, which was a frequent complaint lodged against realistic novels, particularly a work written in first-person dialect such as Mark Twain's *Adventures of Huckleberry Finn*. Only with post-Hemingway critical vision do we recognize the value of such innovations. Dreiser is now recognized, as did a handful of early critics, as one of the first users of the real language of the Midwest, in company with George Ade. Drouet's advice to Carrie, "you stick to me" (60), is colloquialism at its most natural. "Sure," for "yes" (75, 81), "dandiest" to praise Carrie (141), "Get Out" for "I don't believe you" (146) are typical as well, of a character such as Drouet, who calls an inattentive husband, a "chump" (103) in one of the novel's most ironic moments. A bum's plea for a dime begins, "Honest to God, Mister" (103). Hurstwood asks to use a " 'phone" (194) and decides that "they can't get on my track till noon" (194). Carrie's show leaving town "shook him up" instead of "upset him" (337), and in the slush, just prior to his suicide, Hurstwood "slopped onward" (363). But even the author's voice uses colloquial language easily; Carrie, abducted by Hurstwood under false pretenses, "swallowed the whole story" (195) for "believed." As noted before, of Carrie's admiration for fashionable women's clothing the author tells us, "It ached her" (228), after describing various "knickknacks" of silver and gold. Social chat is "self-interested palaver" (36). Such formulations are distinctly midwestern and colloquial, innovations in the language used by novelists, and well removed from the language of the Bertha Clay and Horatio Alger novels. *Hill's Manual*, in fact, lists 170 such brief phrases to be avoided, subtitling them as "MISTAKES in GRAMMAR which are OFTEN HEARD" (Hill, 56–57). Dreiser's language confronts his readers with the unaccustomed usages of a lower social class. Ellen Moers's fine article "The Finesse of Dreiser" describes the importance of this style: "For Dreiser has set himself the task of making Carrie sufficiently null to skirt moral criticism, but vital enough to personify the creative force itself—to be, in effect, his Emma Bovary."[3] The play of commonplaces against other sorts of language achieve this effect. Warmth-cold-sun metaphors, for example, dominate the scene in which Drouet first seduces Carrie into taking money, and "language . . . in turn gives a surprising eloquence to this tawdry encounter between trivial personalities" (Moers 1963, 114). But it is often the simplest of choices of spoken dialect.

At a higher social level, the language continues to be suggestively idiomatic. From Jessica Hurstwood we learn that a family is "poor as church mice" (65). Even more glaring is the author's statement that Drouet could be "hornswoggled" as easily as any silly girl (49). The crucial trait limiting the character is combined with the colloquial vulgarity. When Hurstwood decides to "size up" Drouet, we find a rare use of quotation marks to designate colloquial language (81). In other places, Dreiser offers clichés to reinforce the commonness of conventional ideas: "He [Drouet] was a splendid fellow in the true popular understanding of the term" (45). It is nevertheless worth distinguishing the speech of Dreiser's characters at its most blatant from the colloquial language found in the characters that populate Edith Wharton's *The Custom of the Country*, published 13 years later. The villainous Elmer Moffatt talks about publishing his "meemo'rs" and sees "a kinder poetic justice" in the "dead sure thing" he has got in sight.[3] Such dialect is too exaggerated for Dreiser's sense of texture. A copy of *Sister Carrie* with the first 69 pages revised in Dreiser's own hand shows, in fact, that he even intended to further soften the "colloquial phrasing" and smooth some of the book's awkward styling, perhaps in response to criticism of the novel.[4] Dreiser's use of colloquialisms is more urbane than Wharton's, despite Wharton's being a more "sophisticated" stylist. The colloquial language of Dreiser's characters was meant to be a less obvious device, and it blends with his own language, grating though it was in 1900 to the more schoolmarmish of his offended critics.

Elsewhere in the novel the language takes on a stilted aspect that is equally representative of a midwesterner forcing higher diction. Dorothy Dudley, Dreiser's friend and first major biographer, provides a particularly illuminating discussion of three different kinds of words used by Dreiser. As examples of the "unceremonial speech of the

Middle West," she cites *nice, swell, palavering, flashy, showy, nobby, dress-suit affair,* and a variety of similar words. Even more valuable is her exploration of the second and third pool of words, prairie language and textbook language:

> He wrote apparently as he talked and thought. When the idiom he had always heard and used seemed too meager to convey his meaning, he trimmed it sometimes with grace-notes from highschool days: *lightsome, halcyon, prancing pair of bays, airy grace, fine feather.* These two were part of that Prairie language; the girls sang them to sweet tunes and people used them for special occasions, letters, and speeches. Perhaps they seemed ultra-innocent to the innocent editors who first refused *Sister Carrie.* It is true, they make a curious blend with the text book language—*formative, affectional, actualities*—in which the story also moves, just as American talk moves in impersonalities, so as not to feel the accusation of neglected personal values. (Dudley, 164)

Dudley treats the language in a social context as a friend and confidante of Dreiser, who responded to a number of points in her biography and even convinced her to alter the title when the book was reprinted. Thus she probably accurately represents Dreiser's sense of his language.

The question of whether Dreiser had ultimate control of his words is a somewhat different issue, although Arthur Henry is known to have altered words that did not mean what Dreiser thought they did. Dreiser uses Victorian terminology, as in such notable phrases as "warmed the cockles of her heart" (44) and "This often happens in the best regulated families" (220), an undeniably Dickensian sentence. Words such as "transpierced" (13), used to describe how docks thrust into a stoneyard, must seem strange to almost any reader—a style that represents the awkward forces depicted in the scene, but nonetheless strange.

References to Carrie as a "half-equipped little knight," which pervade the novel from the second page on, may appear to be a particularly exaggerated case of inappropriately sentimental clichés. Arun Mukherjee, however, has shown that metaphors of knights and pilgrims were applied heavily to business enterprise and success in later nineteenth-century America by spokesmen for American business. For example, Francis Hodgeson Burnett's *Two Little Pilgrims' Progress* (1895) shows two young entrepreneurs trying to reach the "city beautiful"—Chicago—in a journey from rags to riches, like Carrie's quest for material wealth in the glitter of the "walled city."[5] The irony is that Dreiser recognizes the language conventions of knight-errantry and shows Carrie as not fulfilling their moral dictates but still triumphing (Mukherjee, 120–23). One may add a book such as Rev. John McDowell Leavitt's *Kings of Capital and Knights of Labor* to Arun Mukherjee's list as another example of Dreiser's expropriating language in a way that is culture-based and intentional. In using the images, however, he is reversing a prevailing cultural stereotype rather than accepting it. Seen in this light, metaphors that would otherwise be hackneyed and stilted are richly ironic and provocative.

Dreiser's special use of the word "thing," the most generalized count noun in the English language, is as important as the colorful metaphors he borrows from sentimental business-oriented romances. In some ways "thing" is a dominant word in the novel. The word does much to deaden sentences in a way that suggests the unintellectual thinking of the characters; as such, it almost takes on the power of metaphor. In chapter 9, for example, amidst a discussion of Carrie's longings and education, Drouet cultivates her love of beauty in these terms: "Drouet heightened her opinion on this and allied subjects in such a manner as to weaken her power of resisting their influence. It is so easy to do this when the thing opined is in the line of what we desire" (76). These evasively flat words make up the language of the seducer; "this . . . such . . . it . . . this . . . the thing . . . what," all deaden the prose style, but all these words impose a sense of authorial dryness toward the sexually suggestive action of the chapter. When Dreiser remarks a page later that "the constant drag of something better was not to be denied" (77), the previously established abstract tone, combined with the distancing effect of the use of the passive voice, takes on the inevitable force of natural law. Likewise, Dreiser seems to be merely reciting facts when he says of Drouet's thrill over pretty women, in the same chapter, "He loved the thing that women love in themselves, grace" (76). Flat though the style seems, it is the very opposite of uninteresting writing.

"Thing" exemplifies Dreiser's use of the abstract to reflect the shallowness of Drouet's and Hurstwood's character. At the moment of Carrie's first great triumph on the Chicago stage, her harrowed lovers are represented by the same word: "Hurstwood resolved a thousand things, Drouet as well" (140). What generalized word could better represent the strength of their devotion and their own limitations of intellect in expressing it? They are neither thoughtful nor articulate men, irrespective of their ability to seduce the weak Carrie. The language used, as much as the words said, demonstrates to us that neither Hurstwood nor Drouet has the penetration to understand that their feelings are derived as much from the theatrical representation—the falseness of the lights and the makeup—as from the real Carrie.

"Thing" shows up elsewhere with the same effect shown above. In the streetcar strike, Hurstwood stolidly feels, "This one trip was a consummate thing" (310). Again on the same page, about his suffering he thinks, "It was a tough thing to have to come to" (310). It is as if Hurstwood is so entrapped in the problems of his existence that he can only grope for an expression and can find no exact words. This explains the credibility of Hurstwood's weak response later to Carrie's desertion, when he mutters only "Left me!" twice and speaks aloud to an empty room, "I tried, didn't I?" (321). Such antiheroic inarticulateness, a profound part of Hurstwood's tragic decline, is made real by its persistence, even while Carrie's increased income at the theater is called a "demoralizing thing" (323).

Growing out of this limited articulateness is a substantial layer of characterization depicting the limited nature of the central characters with the same flat diction. As early as chapter 5 Dreiser advises us that men gathering in Hurstwood's bar "must be explained upon some grounds," possibly "a strange bundle of passions and vague desires give rise to such a curious social institution" (35–36). Perhaps, he suggests, it is "the false ambition of the minds of those so affected" (36). Only a chapter later, Carrie is defined similarly: "Her imagination trod a very narrow round" (39). But the narrow round of the Hanson apartment is soon infected with "the contagion of thought," and there are "thoughts in the air which left disagreeable impressions" (39, 43). Dreiser's method is to leave undefined the finer points of dissatisfaction. Meanwhile, if we can take chapters 5 and 6 as representative, Dreiser focuses on the instinctual instead of the intellectual. Carrie senses things in a man's look that frighten her, but she responds out of her loneliness to the "brotherly" Drouet with his flashing gold rings, which suggest the style for which she yearns. Ellen Moers has commented on the absence of dialogue between Carrie and Drouet when the salesman first slips her money. The articulateness of the scene lies in the actions as described by Dreiser; the characters themselves are too limited in understanding to formulate their ideas fully or put them into speech. Only this hollowness of style gives credibility to later character analysis, such as the statement, "Carrie had loneliness and this mood of her husband. . . . It was a grievous thing. She became restless and dissatisfied, not exactly, as she thought, with Hurstwood, but with life" (242). Readers must struggle with the syntax to determine if Dreiser is telling us that Hurstwood is secondary to a broader force, and it appears that "life" is the broader source of dissatisfaction.

Dreiser's raveling up of combinations of motives in awkward involutions and flat words mirrors the confusion within his characters. The style here appears to be a strength rather than a weakness in mirroring character and mood that are consistent with the novel's ideology. Lawrence Hussman goes so far in attacking some of Dreiser's metaphors that his complementary analysis of style is worth noting: "Dreiser was often sloppy in his diction and grammar. He was always after bigger game than pronoun antecedents." Hussman goes on to suggest that Dreiser was "not in total control of the abstract ideas with which he intended to explain Carrie's motivations."[6] Style does override ideas and in some ways muddies them, but this is finally appropriate to their complexity.

The discussion of style can be broadened in yet another way given the literary conventions of the period in which Dreiser wrote. Critic Sandy Petrey sees three levels of style in *Sister Carrie* derived from the conventional literature of the period. Dreiser uses the sentimental partly as a burlesque, partly seriously, but with the overall intention of establishing his opposition to contemporary morality. Petrey argues convincingly that Dreiser exaggerates stylistic conventions of the fiction of his day, particularly. The style ranges from the stripped reportorial style of his action sequences to the labored philosophy and sentiment of interjected passages that comment on, rather than portray, the action. These styles, Petrey contends, have a marked effect on the reader's response to the novel and the problems of the characters within the plot: "By severing the language of realism from the language of sentimentality. . . . Moral concerns appear only in a grotesque form. . . . the depiction of American life as it is lived periodically vanishes and is replaced by another kind of writing, that favored by those committed to American morality as it is proclaimed" (Petrey, 104). What critics describe as Dreiser's "brooding presence" may derive from this mix of styles from flatly didactic to Minnie's dream sequence of Carrie's fall to the author's reflective tone when considering the influence of animal instincts and behavioral drives, to the immediacy of descriptive action in short sentences barren of sentiment.

Dreiser's style also provides the alchemy by which he transforms the moral into the bad and undesirable component of Carrie's life and makes the immoral not only less than evil but even a preferred alternative. This is particularly apparent in Carrie's interactions with sister Minnie and the whole Hanson relationship that inducts us into the world of the novel. At that point in the novel, not only does Dreiser take a number of paragraphs to offer moral speculations, he also uses his splendid awkwardness to turn ideas of conventional morality upside down. On the first page of the novel, Dreiser contends that when a girl leaves home at 18, "either she falls into saving hands" or "assumes the cosmopolitan standard of virtue and becomes worse" (1). The statement is apparently clear, but the word "fall" is linked to saving, and virtue is the bad alternative! Likewise, after a lengthy sociological paragraph on the seductive potential of the "human hives" of the city, which "has its cunning wiles, no less than the infinitely smaller and more human tempter," something like disembodied sin speaks to Carrie as "a voice in her ear," pointing out in commonplace slang "one of the prettiest little resorts in Wisconsin." The shift from abstract to local is arresting. Nonetheless, "the daring and magnetism of the individual, born of past experiences and triumphs, prevailed." The descriptive language is ambiguous as to whether Drouet will be a sin-stained villain or a chivalric hero. Forces of vice seem attached to the social milieu rather than to the man.

In analyzing the novel we may want to consider that the brooding omniscient author is purposely moving beyond the conventional categories of "omniscient author" or "third-person limited narrator-character." In *Sister Carrie*, Dreiser has broken loose from the conventions governing these possible authorial roles by describing the characters from an omniscient third-person viewpoint. Dreiser calculatedly limits this omniscient voice to only identifying the well-springs of human behavior. As Sandy Petrey rightly points out, Dreiser uses a different style of writing when he discusses philosophical issues or describes background. He intrudes into the story so frequently, in fact, that his way of becoming a part of the action of the novel differs from that of most realist authors. In one example Petrey compares the use of money in the first paragraph of chapter 7 where the language is relatively elaborate regarding Carrie, describing "one of her order of mind"—"cast away upon a desert island with a bundle of money, and only the long strain of starvation would have taught her that in some cases it could have no value" (48)—to the despairing Hurstwood's simple "I was all right. I had money" (361) in the concluding chapter. However, in the earlier lines, Dreiser is particularly clear on his intentional use of this format: "As for Carrie, her understanding of the moral significance of money was the popular understanding, nothing more" (48). Explaining the conventional, pompous phraseology is Dreiser's conscious resort—his realistic reflection of the world of 1900 in its own language. He is not writing a caricature in this particular paragraph, and this explanation is important to our understanding of Carrie, for he is merely borrowing from the social milieu surrounding her.

Philosophical discussions are so much a part of the story that the "mind" of the author intrudes openly into the reader's sense of the action. What will the author say to carry on his dialogue with us about the lives of the characters? Dreiser makes use of both a very new and a very old narrative storytelling form in which the teller makes no pretense of hiding but places himself in relation to the reader.[7] Because Dreiser does this, his work takes on a quality much different from that of the realists and naturalists who attempted not to intrude so obviously into their stories. We can also say that the narrator's analysis becomes part of the tension of the story—*not* merely as a point of view that should be taken seriously but as a dramatic element. The ponderously didactic written passages become more important than the fluent passages passing without notice. Petrey is right to conclude that the passages are important in their stylistic differences, and we can go even further in interpreting their likely effect on a reader. When Sherwood Anderson used overtly groping authorial explications and an exaggerated style to make his questioning a tool in his fiction, critics were quick to pillory his method, calling him a "corn-fed mystic." Dreiser's groping style has likewise been critiqued as a somewhat inept affectation, but this is the narrow view of it.

Petrey offers another valuable insight to explain the exaggerated sentimental language of the chapter titles, drawing on Phillip Williams's study of the titles.[8] Williams, she notes, contends, "The clash between the mellifluous drivel of most titles and the social realism of their chapters is more evident because of the presence of a single descriptive title, chapter 41's 'The Strike'. Two syllables instead of anapestic tetrameter, a socially charged term rather than a sentimental dictionary" (Petrey, 109). Although the chapter titles were a late addition to the manuscript, we might also remember that when Doubleday attempted to change the book's title to "The Flesh and the Spirit," Dreiser changed it back to "Sister Carrie." This suggests that Dreiser knew what he was doing in the matter of headings and titles and that he accepted the exaggerated rhetoric of the chapter titles to counterpoint with the text, although he did not wish the whole story to be identified with this rhetoric. It is ultimately quite reasonable, although untidy from the standpoint of the modern critic, to assume that Dreiser saw the titles in two or three different ways, including using the titles as both ironic commentary and a justifiable and truthful sentimental exaggeration of the experience portrayed.

As with the chapter titles, the long passages of interpolated scientism, psychology, and moral philosophy, and even the interjected "alas" and "O, Carrie" are obvious intrusions of specific styles that carry alternate viewpoints of the action. For an instance of a true breach of style—which is much rarer than most critics claim—one might look at the "Sun" review of Carrie's performance as the little Quakeress. The third sentence portrays the fictive event as exactly the reverse of how it was described in the narrative, with Carrie totally unnoticed in act 1. The final sentence does not belong in a review as much as in the authorial context, and the writing seems incredibly forced: "It is a bit of quiet, unassuming drollery which warms like good wine. Evidently the part was not intended to take precedence, as Miss Madenda is not often on the stage, but the audience, with the characteristic perversity of such bodies, selected for itself. The little Quakeress was marked for a favourite the moment she appeared, and thereafter easily held attention and applause. The vagaries of fortune are indeed curious" (326–27). The blending of the newspaper reviewer's column with Dreiser's authorial voice is possibly done on purpose, to help us see an oddity in the reviewer's understanding and portrayal of what he criticizes. The final line actually seems more like a mistaken inclusion than anything else.

Hurstwood's foreshortened response to Carrie's success becomes one of the most brilliant dramatic counterpoints of the novel when in this chapter (43) Carrie's salary is elevated from $30 to $150, and Hurstwood, reading the same newspaper, declares, "Well, let her have it, I won't bother her." Dreiser adds, "It was the grim resolution of a bent, bedraggled, but unbroken pride" (328). Hurstwood's truculent, tragic words and the limited language of the narrator make Hurstwood's spirit rise in proportion to his loss of status and wealth, true to tragic form. In contrast, the verbiage and the superficial expressions of the reviewer describing Carrie's ascendance show us that he has not penetrated the appeal of Carrie's spirit in relation to her rise to success. Although we are aware of the intrusion of another style, the review inadvertently confirms our feelings about Carrie. So the awkward element is not merely failed writing; it is part of the novel's machinery for bringing about a response in the reader.

In a more obvious way the dream sequences announcing Carrie's fall to her sister Minnie bear on this discussion. When Minnie dreams of Carrie's fall, it has been suggested that Dreiser either has committed a massive breach of style or is satirizing the sentimental novel. Neither premise is exactly correct. Minnie's melodramatic dreams of Carrie's descent not only foreshadow Dreiser's extensive use of the same imagery for Hurstwood's decline (death sequences in imagistic language), but they also establish the antagonism between our real heroine Carrie and the false sentimentalizations of those who operate in the limited realm of the conventional. Minnie's Dickensian conventionalities of melodramatized moral rectitude would have to be dramatized in a luridly symbolic vision of what Carrie is about to do. The images and language used to describe them are true to the mind of the character who dreams them and the society she represents. In fact, the threat is real; Carrie, "fallen," cannot return. In Dreiser's realistic story of the "fall" of a young girl entitled "Old Rogaum and His Theresa," which is of the same vintage as *Carrie*, Dreiser had developed the same theme. In the depiction of a father, old Rogaum the butcher, Dreiser does not need to use a dream sequence because the language of the short story is realistic and appropriate. But the melodrama of Minnie's dream depicts a broad sociological situation better than would a flatly realistic description, and because the novel presents a wider range of worldly philosophies than does the short story, Dreiser has calculated his use of a sentimental style to bring Minnie's kind of thinking to life.

Carrie's rocking chair is often discussed as the novel's chief symbol, and there is little need to spend much time on it, but it must be mentioned in passing here. Carrie returns to the rocking chair again and again to brood on her fate. Likewise, as Hurstwood becomes overwhelmed by events, he also becomes bound by the rocking chair—a perfect symbol of motion without outcome, because it rocks but does not progress. The rocking chair is another seemingly Dickensian device, used far more obviously than the tenets of good realistic writing might allow. Carrie returns to her rocking chair to sing and dream at the end of the novel. Hurstwood, however, has occupied a corresponding seat while reading his newspaper with its tide of events nurturing his forgetfulness. The chair has gathered fuller associations by virtue of belonging to both major characters. As Hurstwood's seat, it has taken on much deeper associations with decline and despair. Thus, even the obvious physical symbols develop in Dreiser's writing the broadest implications that can be shared among the characters.

The suggestion is sometimes made that Dreiser falls "unconsciously" into the style of the nineteenth-century sentimental novel, but Sandy Petrey's analysis should convince us otherwise. We can conclude that Dreiser drops into that style because it represents the thinking of the milieu of his characters, and he intends to make his readers encounter those attitudes. If we disallow the characters' milieu, the life Dreiser portrays becomes substantially less mysterious. It is crucial that the conventional ideology be presented by the characters in their own language; otherwise, where is the tension between the characters and the world they inhabit? Without the stylistic alterations, Dreiser's philosophical positions would not be nearly so well dramatized.

The business metaphors of knight-errantry, as Mukherjee suggests, provide another range of clichés bearing an implicit ironic comment on the intellectual and cultural assumptions that the novel attacks. Even as we see the first true antiheroes, we hear them speaking in antirhetorical flatness and even observe the author describing the musing flat words repeatedly to reflect their limitations. At the same time, the author retains the ideas of sentiment and convention in their own place, couched in their own rhetoric. Through style, Dreiser escapes the necessity of constantly reminding us of the limitations placed on his heroes by the social conventions of the world they inhabit. Dreiser as much as any author in American literature may be credited with developing a style appropriate for the postrealistic novel of the twentieth century. Dos Passos would be more obvious in his use of stylistic variations in *U.S.A.*, Wolfe more floridly emotional in *Look*

Homeward, Angel; Dreiser himself would multiply pages of dry descriptions in later novels, and so a host of other novels would follow *Sister Carrie* in developing styles specially fitted to their subject matter, the awkwardly new and diverse world of twentieth-century America. But *Sister Carrie* seems a first.

7

The Sociological Metaphor and Other Imagery

THE SOCIOLOGICAL METAPHOR

Naturalism, like realism before it, pretends to present the truthfulness of life, and Dreiser in "True Art Speaks Plainly" took this position. Dreiser's intention, "To express what we see honestly and without subterfuge: this is morality as well as art,"[1] was relatively radical for 1903, particularly given that he applied it in *Sister Carrie*, providing in it the overpowering weight of social, physical, and moral observation and commentary. Dreiser's use of descriptive detail serves a literary function that both furthers the readers' sense of reality where conventional moral standards break down and builds their feeling of the novel's overpowering reality. Particularly, the use of city imagery develops a sociological context for the characters. The *American Heritage Dictionary* supplies this definition of *sociology*: "The study of human social behavior. . . . The analysis of a social institution or societal segment as a self-contained entity or in relation to society as a whole." To some extent, the use of animal imagery is a naturalist alternative to attempt to fulfill this function, but the intrusiveness of details of city life establishes a sociological metaphor that defines the human condition of Dreiser's characters in much more mundane terms. The extent to which Dreiser relies on the imagery of urban life to establish his context figures significantly in the sense of "reality" that so many contemporary critics found in his work. As noted before, on almost any page of *Sister Carrie* Dreiser presents compelling material that generalizes social behavior or typifies contemporary artifacts and characters. He creates a metaphor for life through his settings and his complex use of descriptive materials to serve several functions in the plot. He describes his characters in terms of his world, claiming for them the importance of "types," and making that world a component in the characterization and caste of mind of those main figures. The city, the factory, and the artifacts of society dominate the story. Examining the editorial changes made on the first page of the novel gives us an unmistakable indication of Dreiser's intent in emphasizing the role of the city as a presence in the story. When several lines were cut from page 1 for the Heinemann London edition, the line that was left from the middle of them was "The city has its cunning wiles no less than the infinitely smaller and more human tempter" (2). This personification of the city is especially valuable because it notifies the readers that a larger social process is at work in the plot along with the characters, and, in some sense, may subsume them.

Philip Fisher has argued in *Hard Facts* that Dreiser created a city where "self-making" is the natural outcome of psychological habits, events, and objects that are part of a new economic experience unlike any that Americans had perceived before Dreiser's time.[2] In such a world, incompleteness and anticipation are characteristic of a world where "[n]either moral choices nor patterns of manner, but careers give the scheme of action" (Fisher, 13). Thus, Fisher calls the city a "synecdoche" for America and the factory a "metonymy" for work (Fisher, 129–32). As parts of an urbanized process Carrie and Hurstwood engage in symbolic actions, such as rocking in a rocking chair, reading the newspaper, and acting, that symbolize their dissociation from themselves, for they are always trapped in a process of becoming something else. Indeed, Fisher asserts that the roles of Hurstwood and Carrie merchandise their selves, so that they become true representatives of a world governed by economics (Fisher, 163). The city becomes the world, the world defines the personalities of the characters, which is a reversal of our usual assumption that the world is made up of individuals. This analysis readily explains why so many critics, at a loss for words, simply identify Dreiser's strength with his ability to tell the truth—to see things as they really are.

A particular problem lies in assessing the degree to which the characters are controlled by external forces or by their own chemistry. In fact, evidence exists on both sides of the case—not surprisingly, since part of Dreiser's argument is that the expression of character, if not character itself, is changed by social and economic environment. Dreiser began the novel by stressing the moral options of the city. Other commentators, speaking in nearly identical terms, had already established these options as options of choice. For example, Edward W. Bok, in "A Country Lad in the City," asserted in 1896, "Men themselves are not one iota worse or better in the city than in the country. . . . A greater number of temptations exist in the city, naturally. These he can accept or reject, just as he sees fit. It depends on the man absolutely."[3] However strong the "drag of desire" may be, Dreiser well knew and may have agreed to some extent with this concept of action. Yet he also argues, in a passage that did not appear in the 1900 text, that "subtleties of life" also account for failures of personality where "severe tests" have been made. Dreiser suggests that his readers could suffer the same failures given equally grim circumstances (Penn, 98). Just below the same statement, Dreiser argues about Carrie and Drouet that "the leading strings were with neither of them" (Penn, 98).

Dreiser is at pains to note here and there in the novel that his characters do have options, but the particular set of characters who occupy the center of the novel are not depicted as capable of choosing the less palatable and more socially accepted paths. The temptations of the city, to which the weak-willed characters succumb, make it a corrupter rather than a savior. Dreiser's treatment of the city as corrupter is based on the literary technique of metaphorization. Donald Pizer has noted that the "city is a symbol of experience" in citing such passages as the moralistic musing by Dreiser that "When a girl leaves home at eighteen, she does one of two things: Either she falls into saving hands and becomes better, or she rapidly assumes the cosmopolitan standard of virtue and becomes worse" (Pizer, 53). Pizer explicates the passage as Dreiser's expression of "life in the guise of the city, which is the universal seducer of mankind" (Pizer, 53). Pizer's summation of his point is noteworthy, for he, too, sees a "metaphoric intent" in the scenes of the city, which establish the emotional logic of Carrie's movement from drabness and toil to the bright lights and material aspirations of the well-to-do. Consequently, sociological inevitability seems to lie behind the most melodramatized action in chapter 8, when "the swirl of life" makes Carrie "the victim of the city's hypnotic influence," because she "had no excellent home principles fixed upon her" (60). "Home" and "city" are countervailing forces that determine the individual's progress; home, the appealing resort of conventional sentimentalists, is the less appealing of the two. As Minnie dreams of Carrie's fall into the pit, the reader feels that two types of power are seducing Carrie: first, the "vibration of force" that emanates from the would-be lover Drouet, and second, the "bare" downtown section that provides the background for his successful efforts to win her. Carrie's later lovers will emit more force, and further cityscapes will become even colder, until, continuing the metaphorical process, the snowy winters of New York City envelop Hurstwood.

Perhaps one of the best examples of the sociological observation used as metaphor is Dreiser's ponderous description of the department store in chapter 3, following the generalized foreshadowing in his description of the city in the previous chapter (12–13). Extensive detailing of the store's emotional effect is provided, with the summary excuse that "the nature of these vast retail combinations, should they ever permanently disappear, will form an interesting chapter in the commercial history of our nation" (17). Chicago's vast and huge energies lead to this grand type of American commercial energy, the department store (16). Critics have often complained that this passage is typical of Dreiser's pompous posing as a social reporter. Dreiser uses the metaphoric power of the city to further characterize the world for which Carrie yearns—"imposing," "bustling," "successful," a "show place of dazzling interest and attraction," full of "trinket[s]," "dainty" women's clothing, "all touched her with individual desire" (17). Not only do they represent a chance for us the readers to study American sociology; the descriptions of the goods offered in the department stores also make Carrie appear "poor and in need of a situation," an "outcast," suffering the "drag of desire" from watching "her more fortunate sisters of the city" (17). Such powerful and important passages do not stand alone: they *fuse* the nature of the world of wealth with the personal yearnings of the heroine. The dazzling extravagances of the world become the material with which Carrie feels. Furthermore, Dreiser egregiously personifies material artifacts, allowing lace collars to speak to Carrie as enticingly as spring daffodils ever spoke to the more sentimental class of nature poets. Certainly, no romantic poet ever used the pathetic fallacy to unite emotion and natural artifact better than Dreiser uses his social observations and the personifications of material objects to embody and project the feelings of Carrie. It would be fair to say that Fitzgerald and Moy's saloon defines Hurstwood similarly. Since Vance Packard's *The Hidden Persuaders* in 1957, Americans have recognized the powerful shaping of personal desires by commercial entrepreneurs using industrial design to stimulate appeal; Dreiser, in using this fictional technique is half a century before his time.

Dreiser expands the sociological metaphor to include descriptions of factory life, which become part of the emotional background of the characters and help to symbolize the world from which Carrie wants to escape. The sociological discussion, with its attendant descriptions, becomes part of the feelings of the characters and the action of the novel in a way that simple description of the surroundings might not. The sordid world of the manufacturing sweatshop (30–31) both describes a setting and gives more characterization of Carrie. The suggestion is made that it is grimy and coarse. Dreiser observes the discomfort of the workers almost clinically and comments, "Under better material conditions, this kind of work would not have been so bad, but the new socialism which involves pleasant working conditions for employees had not then taken hold upon manufacturing compa-

nies" (30). Carrie is poked in the ribs, accosted with rude propositions (although substantially less rude in print than was the original
manuscript in its depiction of the sexual overtures of prospective employers, shown in the Pennsylvania edition); and she "instinctively
withdrew into herself" to avoid the lowness (30). Further, the "machine girls" seem "common" to Carrie, and their slang and dress are
"hardened by experience" (40). Illness ends her brief tenure as a factory girl. The metaphor of factory life for failure, however, returns
strongly at the end of the novel, again used by Dreiser to stress the
inability of Carrie to escape from the specter of want that Hurstwood
has come to embody for the reader. Plot and setting merge here into
something larger: they become the mental landscape of the reader,
who will recapture more of the generalized feeling from Dreiser's
description of Hurstwood's decline into such circumstances than by
explicit reminiscence at the one or two points where Carrie restates
her early experience.

The second reference to the factory occurs in chapter 8 (59). Just
after Drouet takes Carrie to one of the great stores—Carson, Pirie's—
to buy new clothes, she shivers with thoughts of home, and Drouet
uncomprehendingly instructs her to wear a "boa about your throat to-
night." Immediately thereafter, she and Drouet encounter chattering
shopgirls on their way home from work—"a spectacle of warm-
blooded humanity." Carrie does an emotional about-face when she
and one of the "poorly dressed girls" recognize one another. Describing the shopgirl's clothing as loose-hanging, old, and shabby, Dreiser
uses the very words that he later applies to Hurstwood's appearance
when he declines to the status of Bowery bum. For Carrie, who senses
a "great tide" between herself and the shopgirls, "The old dress and
the old machine came back." When she starts, and then bumps a
pedestrian, the oblivious Drouet only remarks, "You must be thinking," without any sense of the enormity of Carrie's thought. Had
Carrie been more literary, she might well have been thinking of
Thomas Hardy's 1866 poem, "The Ruined Maid":

> "You left us in tatters, without shoes or socks,
> Tired of digging potatoes, and spudding up docks;

And now you've gay bracelets and bright feathers three!"—
"Yes: that's how we dress when we're ruined," said she.[4]

But whereas Hardy's comic heroine is delighted and crows cockily about her ruination, Carrie, by contrast, is startled by the glance and haunted by the full look of the factory girl. Hurstwood, too, "fears the publicity of it" (94) and escapes, in a passive wording, "when a livery stable sign in one of the side streets solved the difficulty for him" (94). Both in plot and in symbol, sociological influences provide levers of action.

The moment is recaptured at the end of the novel to reinforce the threat of social experience to happiness. Carrie's knowledge of Chicago sweatshops is brought back to her and to the reader as a powerful statement of alternatives hanging over her. The power of social "fact" explains, even if it does not justify as fully as Dreiser wishes it to, the inevitability of the course Carrie chooses (368). The world of the shoe factory is for Carrie the alternative to her wishes for a life responding to "the great, mysterious city which was still a magnet for her" (50). The shoe factory appears at three points in the story, and each time it reinforces its lesson. First, it condemns the world of lower-class drudgery dictated by the narrow morality of the Hansons. Second, it provides a brief, chilling contrast on Carrie's "fall" (59). Third, it haunts her on the occasion of her first large paycheck with her Broadway success—a moment at which she comes to realize loneliness of spirit just as Hurstwood begins the fully realized loneliness of his final decline to suicide. We are told in chapter 44 that just as Carrie notices the new courtesy of the clerk when he hands her her enlarged $150 salary and his curtness to an "insignificant member" who follows, "She knew that out in Chicago this very day the same factory chamber was full of poor homely-clad girls." Carrie's catalog of their workday follows: they were "working in long lines at clattering machines; . . . at noon they would eat a miserable lunch," to which she responds, "Oh, it was so easy now!" (334). Dreiser claims that Carrie is thrilled, but I suspect that the recollection actually depresses the reader as Dreiser intended, for he follows this passage immediately with a description not of happiness but rather of Carrie's loneliness. Lola suggests that Carrie spend more time with the available men, and Carrie returns to looking out at "the passing crowd," a further strong suggestion of her isolation, which Dreiser has suggested from the first moment that she withdraws within herself in the face of the factory experiences. The stark counterpoint of the reminiscence parallels the larger counterpoint in the plot between Carrie's rise and Hurstwood's decline. Thus one component of the story includes the language and implications of the overall tragedy, even while it pretends to be merely a character's passing reflection.

Hurstwood's thinking is colored for us much as Carrie's is—by the social context that forms the substance of his impressions and responses. Only in terms of a broad sociological process does it make sense for Hurstwood to think "that he saw at once that a mistake had been made" (91) in Carrie's social position. Although this is a rather abstracted social comment, Dreiser has established a framework of social relationships that suggests proper spheres for the participants; "difficult conditions" and "sympathy" are thus elicited by dint of some seeming wrong in the social scale. Several critics have pointed out that Dreiser actually shows a large amount of human freedom and sympathy within the seemingly inhumane natural and social laws he depicts.[5] Such a response by Hurstwood, even the initial response of Drouet to some extent, are examples of their refusal to submit to their milieu. Coarse though Hurstwood and Drouet are implied to be, this particular moment of attraction is based on Hurstwood *not* seeing the art and calculation of mistress or courtesan in Carrie. Carrie is "worth loving if ever youth and grace are to command that token of acknowledgment" (107) as Dreiser tells us, and even in writing love notes to her, Hurstwood (in the remarkable chapter 15, which does so much to place the affair within a larger social environment) causes his "five bartenders [to view] with respect the duties which could call a man to do so much desk-work and penmanship" (106).

At times this social environment can rise into the melodramatic, as it does in the New York section of the novel where Hurstwood's economic fortune is in decline. Dreiser is able to magnify and intensify the significance of the details of such trifling activities as buying a newspaper and visiting the grocer, achieving a domestic melodramatization of Hurstwood's battle against circumstances, punctuated, however, by real warfare in the streetcar strike. The overt warfare of "McEwen of the Shining Slave Makers" is not fully appropriate, so Dreiser transfers this urgency to domestic detail by noting the problem in paying for butcher, grocer, and newspaper. Some of the language raises the level of tension but maintains the domestic context: "The game of a desperate man had begun" (288) is typical of these sorts of summaries, this one capping Hurstwood's first deferment of a payment to Oeslogge the butcher. This is followed by the "extension of the credit system in the neighborhood" (290). The economy of half-dollars and measures of flour bags is a grandiose trivialization of the events to which Hurstwood—once wielding the social power of a Roman senator—is reduced.

Odd though it may seem, even the tendency to intrude seemingly irrelevant details into the action helps define the emotional action as involved with layers of supra-personal experience (194). Dreiser's mentioning that Hurstwood calls from one of Chicago's first phone booths to check train times for his escape with the stolen money is one example. The telephone reference is slight, but it reminds us of the intrusion everywhere of historical and social fact, foreshadowing later critical manipulations of the reader's sense of Carrie's world. For example, in chapter 43, Carrie is catapulted into affluence by chance, beginning with a "wee notice" (322) from the Sunday reviewer. Dreiser tells us, "It was about that time that the newspapers and magazines were beginning to pay that illustrative attention to the beauties of the stage which has since become fervid" (322), and Dreiser adds further details that directly foreshadow the notices Carrie will receive. This later sociological commentary colors our understanding of Carrie's success, making it clear that far larger social forces worked by chance in Carrie's favor. References like the telephone passage validate this kind of observation later.

The device expands into plot action as Carrie's friend Lola assures her that she will get further notice, because "you do better than most that get theirs in now" (323). The changing needs of the papers and the society they represent will reward Carrie's labor partially by the mere course of events. The ultimate importance of trying to conceive of a new form of realist-naturalist metaphor in which social change replaces natural beauty lies here. Chance social factors have major impact on the realism of the plot. Needless to say, Dreiser makes clear that the lust of the male audiences who view her is a major component in her success. Reviewers again and again commented on the truthfulness to observed fact in Dreiser's novel, and the wedding of historical observation and plot events accounts for this quality in the book. This was the message conveyed in such sequences as the Wellington Hotel's solicitation of Carrie for her publicity value in chapter 44. The lives of the central characters are deeply influenced by their milieu, and the kinds of descriptions here labelled sociological metaphors link characters and environment.

Treating the central male figures as types expands the sociological feeling of the novel into characterization. Dreiser makes a show of relying on social description very heavily in the first few pages of the novel in introducing his characters. Carrie is "a fair example of the middle American class" (2), and Drouet is "a type of the travelling canvasser for a manufacturing house—a class which at that time was first being dubbed by the slang of the day 'drummers' " (3). There follows the close description of dress and character type, punctuated by such phrases as "for the order of intellect represented" and "lest this order of individual should permanently pass" (3). So aggressive was Dreiser in pursuing the actuality that there followed the plagiarized sequence from George Ade's *Fables in Slang*, in which the rudely familiar "Gus" from St. Paul, Minnesota, uses his skills in picking up women in department stores and on trains to woo and win Myrtle, leaving the more conservative mandolin-playing suitors "backed into a Siding" like a hired orchestra. Dreiser borrowed the manner and even the wording for the lengthy passage that defines Drouet as the "masher" type.

When Hurstwood is introduced, he is also defined as a type. He is referred to as "the manager" long after he has absconded from his managership at Fitzgerald and Moy's. Dreiser also tags his character initially with a generalized description: "Hurstwood was an interesting character after his kind" (33). Surrounded by the glitter of cut glass, the blaze of lights, and the company of good fellows and good times, he "was altogether a very acceptable individual of our great American upper class—the first grade below the luxuriously rich" (34). Here, as elsewhere, the sociological comment does more to characterize Hurstwood than the other way around; it infuses the character with his importance and allows us to identify his other traits more than it lends him any air of being either a type or an abstraction. Thus the sociological metaphor adds dimensions to individuals that will later help us to understand their thinking and explain their actions, or lack of action in the case of the despairing and isolated Hurstwood.

Hurstwood, like Carrie, is subject to the power of the urban setting in an extension of his social surroundings to his own status. In Chicago, he is of the "would-be *gilded*" attempting to rub off gilt, leaning toward notabilities. Too proud to toady, he is nonetheless involved in "those pointless social conversations so common in American resorts," and when the "social flavour" is strong enough, he would drink glass for glass with his associates (189). These kinds of metaphors further define the characters to a significant extent. When Hurstwood contemplates his relationship to Carrie in chapter 13, the highly implicative language recurs. At first heavily figured rhetoric—"he knew of that underworld where grovel the beast-men of society"—dominates, as Dreiser illuminates the "moil of the city" into which "maidenhood" has wandered (91). At the same time, however, Hurstwood's mind is likened to that of an Irish saloon keeper in the Bowery (Dreiser is already switching his metaphors to New York). From a combination of personal desire and the natural experience of the city Hurstwood comes to his one abrupt realization about Carrie: "He saw at once that a mistake had been made, that some difficult conditions had pushed this troubled creature into his presence, and his interest was enlisted" (91). Expressed in a passive construction, the idea is part of the sociology that pervades the plot. As a plot event, furthermore, Hurstwood's reaction to Carrie perfectly foreshadows the responses of all other men who witness her performances both in *Under the Gaslight* in Chicago and as the little Quakeress in New York. The addition of sentimental language—speaking freely of "virtue in the toils"—involves and enlarges the prevailing moral ideologies in the scene. The language reflects the period more than it is an ironic rejection of its ideology.

This morality extends to Hurstwood, for the evils of drink reflect the drag of society on Hurstwood's spirit as much as the drag of material goods pulls Carrie. Thus made "warm in his fancies," albeit still clear headed, by the social conditions that constitute his environment and the physically roseate state that the socially prompted drinking induces, Hurstwood, in his tragic moment of weakness, finds the safe open and removes his employers' money. Hurstwood's vice derives from an abstract social desire. His "moral revulsion" closely follows the theft, and he identifies the moment accurately as "but a single point in a long tragedy" (210). He later feels accused without being understood, and, adrift without status in the world, he is in a parallel position to Carrie's early in the novel, but he lacks her youthful innocence and energy. New York's oceanic multiplicity has shorn him of all the pleasantries of his life; he has been "cut off from friends, despoiled of his modest fortune, and even his name, and forced to begin the battle for place all over again. He was not old, but he was not so dull but he could feel he soon would be" (215). The tragedy of economic separation from "all that he most respected on this earth—wealth, place, and fame" has begun, and Hurstwood is disabled by the loss of the social moorings that have given his life its consistency. Unlike Carrie, he faces the specter of age and weakness as an additional problem. He now cruises the city, looking at the "mass of buildings erected" (319) much as Carrie had entered her first great city—as the structure of the plot now completes its cycle, the artifacts of humanity overshadow the characters.

A last sociological metaphor is worth noting, the anti-feminine stereotyping associated with some wealthy but trivial dissipations. From early on, the "drag" of desire for clothing is peculiarly attached to Carrie as a woman (13, 17, 77), for when she wears poor clothes, fine ladies ignore her. Dreiser connects her desire for fine clothes with her sex when he tells us that she made the average feminine distinctions about the quality and richness of clothes (31). Drouet, in a passage that expands on this instinctualism, is described as "vain, he was boastful, he was as deluded by fine clothes as any silly-headed girl" (49). So men may share in traits of weakness, but female sexual traits, human and animal nature, and city life and social experience combined explain how the chief characters respond to their world. Partly, we may be experiencing an echo of Dreiser's feelings about Sister Emma, or perhaps merely the nascent sexism of the era, but the implication is to add one more degrading or dragging force to life, and to the heroine—compared to which her nonintellectual sensitivity is the positive side.

OTHER IMAGERY

Sociological metaphors that make the very geography and architecture of the city into the emotional atmosphere of the characters are not the only symbolic representations of the novel, of course. The reader also encounters the more typical metaphors of naturalism in the animal and scientific metaphors that Dreiser, like other sterner realists—Jack London and Frank Norris—used as their focal points. Dreiser focuses on the weakness of human will set against the moral precepts that poverty invalidates. Consequently, he convincingly works animal habits and chemical tropisms into his agenda and into the texture of his novel.

Ellen Moers, in *Two Dreisers* (particularly 160–70) was the first to open up the inquiry into the direct and seemingly profound influence of the scientist Elmer Gates on Dreiser. Dreiser was much impressed when he visited Gates at his laboratory in February 1900. Moers describes Gates as a "physiological psychologist" (Moers 1969, 161) and credits him with much of Dreiser's "confident haste" in writing the description of the decline of Hurstwood—a decline that freely mixes psychological and physical characteristics. Moers's analysis explains one of the most awkward-seeming insertions in the novel's philosophy—the "katastates-anastates" passage explaining Hurstwood's physiological breakdown in chapter 33. Moers contends that Gates's philosophy caused Dreiser to identify "chemical reagents" coloring man's soul (chapter 30). Dreiser later describes the cancer eating at Hurstwood's soul and adds to this scientific diagnosis both a human and a sociological strand: "A distillation not only of his [Hurstwood's] lack of strength and his mediocre brain, but of the day and the city and the circumstances . . . out of Chicago and so away from all he had known and prized."[6] Even science takes on the coloring of the character's humanity and his relation to society as the two are compounded in Dreiserian rhetoric.

In composing *Sister Carrie* Dreiser had to explain why Hurstwood would enter into decline involving a profound loss of identity and self-esteem after taking the money from the safe at Fitzgerald and Moy's. Gates's physiological psychology offered Dreiser a ready explanation in the theory of the effect of "chemisms" on the body. According to that theory, depression breaks down the body by releasing "katastates" or destructive chemicals into the body. This explanation appears at the beginning of chapter 30, and Dreiser returns to it in chapter 33 with a full discussion of katastates and anastates in Gatesian terms. As with the city, external influences effect the weak wills of human actors by becoming internal forces that the characters' wills cannot control. Body chemistry is added to the weight of poverty. Although a passage such as the "katastates" passage can be a philosophical or factual mish-mash, it still is potent in communicating the most significant contention that underpins the entire novel: that poor people feel the compulsion of their situation even more keenly than those intellectually or economically better off. Such insights have a powerful cumulative effect even though the reader may rebel against the author's reasoning. This is one of those places where a dialogue exists not between the characters but rather between the author and reader, advancing the story's real "action" in ways that much literary criticism is ill-adapted to recognize. This passage establishes the feeling of inevitability surrounding Hurstwood's defeat. The immediate causes are the cold and the antagonism of strikers during the winter streetcar strike. The implacable external forces are added to cancerous internal ones stimulated out of broader social experience.

Animal images and sociological descriptions are frequently brought together to illuminate the action. In chapter 30 Dreiser likens Hurstwood to an "inconspicuous drop" in an ocean, a "common fish" among whales—"nothing" (214). Thus, Dreiser reduces Hurstwood to an animal by means of a physical metaphor, whereas the manager had been "a vessel, powerful and dangerous" (160) as late as chapter 22. The author then moves to a discussion of the forces motivating the "tragedies of the world" (214), his first revelation of the novel's true tragic intent. These forces are the effect of the "atmosphere" of the great, with their "magnificent residences," "splendid equipages," and gilded shops, on the small: "So long, also, will the atmosphere of this realm work its desperate results in the soul of man. It is like a chemical reagent. One day of it, like one drop of the other, will so affect and discolour the views, the aims, the desire of the mind, that it will thereafter remain forever dyed. A day of this to the untried mind is like opium to the untried body. A craving is set up which, if gratified, shall eternally result in dreams and death" (214). Dreiser concludes that opium addiction is a metaphor for the ultimate social fall, and Hurstwood will eventually sink into a stupor that reflects that dissolution. Perhaps the various insect metaphors—butterflies, moths, spiders—are intended to increase our sense of physical science and instinctual behavior, as motifs controlling human action, bringing these various strands of reference together, and they do achieve this purpose.

The Miltonian idea of the weakness of untried virtue is so easily mixed with the chemical metaphor that it is almost as easy to miss the one doctrine as it is to overlook what Richard Lingeman has pointed out: Dreiser incorrectly applies the idea of a reagent, having the reagent discoloring the views of man as an actor rather than merely reflecting the change of views by precipitating a color (Lingeman, 265). Passivity and activity thus occupy an uneasy relationship to each other, coexisting in the novel.

The Sociological Metaphor and Other Imagery

Dreiser's presentation moves through the sociological metaphor to the scientific one and finally in the third paragraph of chapter 30 to Hurstwood himself, cordoned off from "all that he most respected on this earth—wealth, place, and fame," and without "the strength of hope which gushes as a fountain in the heart of youth" (215). "Forced to begin the battle for place," he recognizes that he soon will be old, finding himself in a "distressing" state. In the final comparison between age and youth Dreiser achieves the feeling of inescapable doom, blaming Hurstwood's personal decline on natural forces generated by the cityscape in a long chain of metaphors brilliantly enveloped in the garish language of the "other" Dreiser—the intrusive, brooding author.

Chapter 33 expands on the metaphoric progress of chapter 30 by exploring the idea of wealth. As Carrie is "rocking and beginning to see" after meeting Ames at the end of the previous chapter, Hurstwood's condition is assessed in an extended discussion of youth and age: "Either he is growing stronger, . . . or he is growing weaker, older, less incisive mentally, as the man approaching old age" (239). Fortune is personified here, and it is also described as "an organism," but a socioeconomic one that draws to itself young minds and wills. Hurstwood, having neither youth nor fortune, is suffering "depression," which he feels but cannot analyze. The "poisons generated by remorse" begin to produce physical deterioration, here explained explicitly by the concept borrowed from Gates. Locked out of the walled city, his youth fades, Carrie resents the cooling of their relationship, and the Warren Street saloon fails to save him. Dreiser's summary offers us three generalized causes for Hurstwood's fall, each one attributing the fall to a socially induced phenomenon: "the disease of brooding," the failure of the "delight of love," and "a commonplace station in life," all compounded by Dreiser as "the misery of things" (239). These conditions put Hurstwood in his most "serious" predicament, which Carrie even recognizes "serious, very serious": "The road downward has but few landings and level places" (244). The explanatory causes and relationships—social, natural, and personal—give the reader the sense of overpowering and inescapable movement determined by

91

forces outside of the control of the spiritually weakened Hurstwood. Man mirrors society; society reflects nature; all reinforce each other in a round of involved influences—the mysticism that critics find at the center of Dreiser's beliefs. Where Aristotle saw the universe as offering infinite possibilities for categorization, the American naturalist author sees the world as a congeries of interinvolved and convoluted relationships partly natural, partly social, partly philosophical, never independent of each other, implicitly or explicitly.

To the mythos of chemic philosophy, Dreiser also adds the more predictable element of naturalist animal imagery to portray man's competition for survival on the biological and natural level, as opposed to the moral level. In this respect, likening characters to animals suggests their failure to rise from social dictates to higher levels of feeling. In abstract discussion, Dreiser falls easily into defining man's nature as a mix of instinct and free will. At the beginning of chapter 8, Carrie is directly explained in terms of the movement in evolution that leaves humans in uncertainty:

> We see man far removed from the lairs of the jungles, his innate instincts dulled by too near an approach to free-will, his free-will not sufficiently developed to replace his instincts and afford him perfect guidance. He is becoming too wise to hearken always to instincts and desires; he is still too weak to always prevail against them. As a beast, the forces of life aligned him with them; as a man, he has not yet wholly learned to align himself with the forces. In this intermediate stage he wavers—neither drawn in harmony with nature by his instincts nor yet wisely putting himself into harmony by his own free-will. (56–57)

Very soon afterwards Dreiser takes a similar position: "If our streets were not strung with signs of gorgeous hues and thronged with hurrying purchasers, we would quickly discover how firmly the chill hand of winter lays upon the heart; how dispiriting are the days during which the sun withholds a portion of our allowance of light and warmth. . . . We are insects produced by heat, and pass without it" (71). Dogs, men, and sparrows are all cited to suggest the animal and instinctual nature of the "labyrinth of ill-logic" (71) that holds Carrie suspended in an immoral social status but a physically acceptable situation with Drouet. The highest praise that can be paid to Carrie as a heroine is that she fully embodies this indeterminacy throughout the novel and consistently reflects Dreiser's general attitude toward humanity.

Animal imagery figures throughout the novel, although often in a way that is less compelling than in the cases just cited. Carrie is first described as having animal instincts of self-protection in the passage comparing her to chipmunks and sheep. Later Mrs. Hurstwood is given similar characteristics. Chapter 22, where she battles with Hurstwood for supremacy over the household, describes her "sniffing change, as animals do danger, afar off" (152). In this case, Dreiser moves off into weather imagery of "thunder-clouds" without expanding on it. The dog reference from Carrie's description earlier recurs to characterize Hurstwood's inability to cope with life changes. Hurstwood is said to have lost his resilience and become no better than a lap-dog, and Hurstwood brings the idea back when he comments on the life of a motorman in a streetcar strike: "This was a dog's life, he thought. It was a tough thing to have to come to" (310); and a few pages later he trudges "doggedly" home in the blizzard (313). Thus, even the character shares the ideology of the author; authorial prose and the texture of life merge. Miss Lola Osborne, Carrie's little soldier-satellite, realizes her dependency in a more feminine cat metaphor, and in a "pussy-like way . . . cling[s] with her soft little claws" (315). The animal imagery conveys the premise that social conditions have produced the not-fully-evolved nature of mankind.

Metaphors advance our sense of the cataclysm in the Hurstwoods' homelife, exploiting the references to "drift" elsewhere attached to Carrie and developing them into a nautical image that becomes one part of the author's narrative. Dreiser establishes a sea metaphor for Hurstwood's family, for instance, by noting that Hurstwood was "all at sea" (106) as to what his children talk about at the dinner table, establishing language that will characterize his final defeat by his wife, when she takes the wind out of his sails and leaves him "rolling and floundering" at the end of chapter 22 (Carrie will become unmoored as a storm-beaten little craft in chapter 23). Of Hurstwood's children, we learn as they defy him and their mother, that their growing natures are independent and selfish, and their actions match their natures, down to the final locking out of Hurstwood from the house and the life of the family: as George fails to gain admission to his house the cabman sees the head of a young woman in an upstairs window. Hurstwood, like Carrie, is moved about by the drift of circumstances intertwined with and influenced by his own actions.

The final impact of all the strands of metaphor in the novel is profound. From the naturalists Dreiser expropriates the animal images that place man within the Darwinian struggle for survival with inborn uncontrollable urges for animal comforts. From the conventional ideology of the day, he draws in the strain of sexist commentary that provides the covetous dimension of Carrie's character. From the realists he borrows the intense and detailed descriptiveness of both physical objects and the urban landscape. Material objects and social forces take the place of nature to provide the emotional atmosphere of the story. Particularly in the case of the depiction of Chicago as an immense sprawling city of tall buildings he creates a powerful envelope for his story. By punctuating his overall metaphor of urban nature with close-up scenes of sparkling glass and bright lights, he creates within one metaphor a second metaphor of success. Thus Dreiser's triumphantly overdrawn sentimental rhetoric—of Hurstwood seeing himself outside the walled city, of Carrie and her friends as "little soldiers," and of Carrie in moments of isolation rocking in her chair—is far more effective than mere ironic overwriting would be. Dreiser interprets the realistic setting and plays a different set of emotions against the frightening starkness of social and economic life, and thus he translates setting into metaphor, using the pretense of sociology to create and define character and foreshadow plot, a use of setting as profound perhaps as only Cooper in the Leatherstocking Saga had achieved before him.[7]

8

Carrie

As a heroine, Carrie has often been relegated to a secondary status by critics who see Hurstwood as more compelling. Yet, although Dreiser gives Carrie a chipmunk brain by early analogy, he later elevates her to great emotional consciousness. Dreiser indicates many times that he does not wish Carrie to be seen as a shrewd genius, but her qualities are nevertheless above the mediocre nonintellectual capacity, as is made clear to readers by the midpoint of the book. Hurstwood's fall actually provides an emotional atmosphere that envelops Carrie and makes her a tragic heroine.

Such is the power of the plot and the sociological, naturalist, and philosophical apparatus of the novel, that in seeking to identify Carrie's character the reader is often distracted by more circumstantial matters. In fact, her character, though limited, is an appealing one. Carrie is certainly not bad in herself. Although Carrie is "interested in her charms" (2) and ambitious to gain material things, Dreiser does not play heavily on Carrie as a golddigger, particularly in the carefully edited 1900 edition. There is little promise of the Carrie Madenda who emerges at the end of the novel in the crudely innocent small-town girl who boards the train with $4 in Columbia City and is casually picked up by the "masher" Drouet on the train. Still, early in the novel, Dreiser has defined an innocent character who will remain essentially reactive and uncynical, except in the matter of approaches from men, for the rest of the book. She begins as a flat-footed and crude second-generation American girl, less than an ingénue of the Daisy Miller sort. She reaches a more advanced level only after succumbing to Drouet's blandishments and gaining exposure to the arts of womanly allure in the boardinghouse, and ultimately in the theatrical performance that marks the terminal point in her development as a desirable young woman in Chicago.

Dreiser did not use many of the dialect characteristics of a lower-class, small-town girl in Illinois. Dreiser's wife, Jug, certainly cleaned up a few inelegances, but Dreiser probably wished to de-emphasize such limiting characteristics, because Carrie needs to be a credible temptation so that a well-to-do upper middle-class manager will leave a more refined family and hazard losing his wealth for her. Also, Carrie's upward mobility needs to be credible. Dreiser makes her "desire" for the good things of the world inarticulate, describing it in the narrative rather than allowing her to speak for herself. Carrie's importance in the scheme of the novel is at least in part that she is a blank personality, reflecting the world rather than shaping it. Ellen Moers notes that in the seduction scene between Carrie and Drouet when money first changes hands between the two, the feelings of the two characters are expressed by attachment to physical things rather than through dialogue between the characters (Moers 1969, 146–50). Critics have commented on how infrequently Carrie actually enters into sustained dialogue, and the reason may lie in the problem of characterization. She really is better off not saying much if she is to be mostly a female principle who both attracts men's lust and contains some degree of emotional greatness.

At the outset Carrie has only "that indescribable thing that made up for fascination and beauty" (5). Carrie's humility is, however, a profoundly appealing quality: she feels a "little ache" for the world of wealth and "her insignificance in the presence of so much magnificence faintly affected her" (5). In sexual matters as well, although Dreiser's real Sister Emma and other women who contributed to the modeling of Sister Carrie presumably had considerable sexual experience, Carrie is described as being relatively artless: "she had not yet learned the many little affectations with which women conceal their true feelings. Some things she did appeared bold. A clever companion—had she ever had one—would have warned her never to look a man in the eyes so steadily" (5).

One of the notable distinctions between the 1900 text and the Pennsylvania restorations is that by the end of the Pennsylvania text, Carrie has indeed learned not to look directly at Ames, and she covers her eyes with her lashes seductively. In the 1900 text such coquettishness does not become a part of Carrie even in success; she never makes the "flutter of an eyelash" that would have brought her male company (283).

Dreiser sets up the emotional feeling for seduction in his narrative very deftly. Such is the case even on the first page. Carrie is designated as "bright, timid, and full of the illusions of ignorance and youth" (1). These relatively noble terms are limited by the preceding description of her clothing, lunch, and portables described as "small" (twice), "cheap," and her destination is written on a "scrap" of paper. This mixture of characteristics foreshadows the seemingly harmless encounter that leads to Drouet's seduction. Alone on the train, Carrie is lured by Drouet, and the drifting young woman, in Dreiser's words, "yielded something" to him. On the first page of the novel Dreiser has already jumped to a more generalized level of discourse in which he opens the seduction theme blatantly. It is quite reasonable to interpret the course of events for Carrie: "When a girl leaves home . . . she falls into saving hands and becomes better, or she rapidly assumes the cosmopolitan standard of virtue and becomes worse" (1). But, as mentioned before, Dreiser uses the phrase "falls into" with "saving hands," confusing what is a fall and what should be a standard of good. "Virtue" linked to "worse" indicates how Dreiser is cleverly manipulative in this statement. Hawthorne created a comparable ambiguity in Hester Prynne in *The Scarlet Letter*, and it is easy to understand why the illustrators of the 1907 Dodge edition of the novel chose a lurid picture of Carrie as a puritan maid—actually the little quaker maid part that brought her her great Broadway break—as the frontispiece for the book. It is no wonder that Carrie, after one suggestive incident, feels "safety and relief in mingling with the crowd" (18). Anonymity is safer than individualism in the flow of forces Dreiser portrays.

As Dreiser describes Carrie, he includes in his general overview astounding language—"perverts" and "weakens"—to describe the effects of "falsehoods" falling on the "unguarded ear" (2). We are then introduced in a second paragraph to "Caroline, or Sister Carrie," who possesses a "mind rudimentary in its power of observation and analysis" with "high, but not strong" self-interest. She is both a "fair example of the middle American class" and two generations removed from emigrants. She is "crude" in the "intuitive graces" but with "native intelligence," otherwise undefined. Dreiser gives and retracts the same characteristics intentionally, throughout the novel, in fact, to show us characters who waver between realities and potentialities. He also foreshadows her fall into vice by describing what evil falls into the "unguarded ear" and then has Drouet speak into "her ear" in the following paragraph, bringing the generalization to the specific character. Dreiser further characterizes her in terms bordering on the mock-heroic: she is a "half-equipped little knight" dreaming dreams of success and wealth in the big city. Carrie is not one type but several types, and her individuality is permanently composed, or some critics might say "compromised," by this threat. Arun Mukherjee has shown that the imagery of knights makes Carrie like a businessman, although clearly less equipped, whose quest is a criticism of the self-congratulatory tone of the period's success literature. Indeed, Carrie's willingness to abandon human ties for business reasons will be a marked feature of her life from this point on—she will become a businesswoman managing her own career, as Philip Fisher contends in *Hard Facts*. Carrie's motifs, however they may be defined, are established fully in the first few pages of the novel.

So quickly do we move from Carrie to descriptions of Drouet, sister Minnie and the Hanson flat that we scarcely notice that we learn about Carrie largely in terms of her responses to others' worlds. Only in chapter 3 do we begin to see Carrie in action: she gains a job in a shoe factory even though her spirit, nurtured in the outdoor countryside of her hometown, revolts against the confinement. Although she feels she is worthy of a higher salary, she tries to convince herself in plaintive internal monologue, filled with suggestive overemphasis, that "she would have a better time than she had ever had before—she would be happy" (21). This action establishes patterns that will be mirrored over and over until the end of the novel, when Carrie's highest search for success is shadowed by her former lover's failure. At no time do we see Carrie as particularly happy. Dreiser takes pains to suggest that she is not in control of her emotions when she is with Hurstwood and Drouet by using the passive voice and intruding such phrases as "she fancied she was," instead of "she was" or "she felt."

Dreiser separates her clearly and flatly from her environment, but often unflatteringly. She looks men directly in the eyes. Her prettiness is "insipid." Ineffectual hands and flat-set feet, and an intellect to match, round out her description. The animal comparisons that make her thinking a labyrinth to her are demonstrated in the superficial variability of her moods in the face of Drouet, the department stores, and the shifting life of the city. Specifically, at the outset, Carrie is designated "not . . . a nervous, sensitive, high-strung nature, cast unduly upon a cold, calculating, and unpoetic world" (17). Of course, even the mentioning of such ideas, even in the negative, allows them some potential, for Carrie will come close to these terms later in some ways. Possibly a few phrases in the Pennsylvania text make her somewhat more vampish, increasing her complicity and making her somewhat more venal and sexual, while making her less of a likable blank screen on which the reader projects sympathy, but the restored material does not significantly alter her relation to the larger forces at work in the world, which determine the actions of people with low incomes and principles of less than rocklike solidity. In fact, both Drouet and Hurstwood underestimate Carrie, and so does almost everyone else. The theatrical manager who would like to "scrape up an acquaintance with her" for his own motives, like the fox of sour grapes to which Dreiser earlier referred, sneers, "She'd never make an actress, though. Just another chorus girl—that's all" (184). Her later loneliness is made more poignant and convincing by these ongoing underestimations.

At the same time that he offers the reader a rather appealing portrait of a modest creature, Dreiser also uses the machinery of the novel to define limitations on Carrie's character that are pronounced:

> She was a work-seeker, an outcast without employment, one whom the average employee could tell at a glance was poor and in need of a situation.
>
> It must not be thought that any one could have mistaken her for a nervous, sensitive, high-strung nature, cast unduly upon a cold, calculating, and unpoetic world. Such certainly she was not. But women are peculiarly sensitive to their adornment.
>
> Not only did Carrie feel the drag of desire for all which was new and pleasing in apparel for women, but she noticed too, with a touch at the heart, the fine ladies who elbowed and ignored her, brushing past in utter disregard of her presence, themselves eagerly enlisted in the materials which the store contained. (17)

Carrie seems less individualized and much more of an abstract social type beginning with the lines of this citation, but she is more personalized in the middle and lower two-thirds of this passage; later she will be singled out as "astonishingly persistent" in her pursuit of work (20). Dreiser describes "her nature to revolt" at the dirt and the "careless and hardened," and presumably "bad-minded and hearted" girls with whom she associates in the first job offered her (19–20). She would like to conform, we feel, to the idealistic vision of the earlier nineteenth century—the vision that was perpetuated in the workinggirl novels of the post–Civil War period, even if the reality of the ideal was dubious at its best and had long since fled in fact, as the melodramatic plots of those novels betray.

Carrie's positive traits lead through sentimental elements in Dreiser's authorial commentary to a self-deluding quality in the heroine. Just after Hurstwood has been introduced and Drouet mentions Carrie, Dreiser calls her "the little toiler" whose "narrow lot" was inseparable from her "unfolding fate" (37). Despite the irony implicit in the overdone sentimentality, such language makes Carrie an object of our sympathy even before she becomes an object for Hurstwood's combined sympathy and lust. Hurstwood is designated as acting out of sympathy in chapter 13, as was Drouet previously. Dreiser never abandons the language of excessive sympathy for Carrie, even though in Bertha Clay's terms Carrie is surviving by disimproving her moral lot. The feelings of others toward her constitutes a motif that relates to men's sexually self-interested moral insensitivity. As is appropriate to the tenets of the school of sterner realism, Carrie's moods, like those of Henry Fleming in Stephen Crane's *Red Badge of Courage*, are driven by circumstances; and Dreiser is at pains to inform us that her feelings change depending on her luck. Thus, when she gets a job offer, "This was a great, pleasing metropolis. . . . She now felt that life was better, that it was livelier, sprightlier" (21). This formulation has an effect on the reader, but it may or may not create sympathy. For some readers, the flight to the language of bathos may be ironic, transforming the novel, or Carrie's "quest" at least, into a travesty. Clearly, for any reader, the sudden change of perspective suggests mental shallowness, but some readers are more harsh than others in their evaluation of the heroine on this basis.

Chapter 11 demonstrates a full panoply of Carrie's appealing qualities and limitations, as Dreiser balances her between attractiveness and limited intellect. Even the first sentence of the chapter is a masterpiece of Dreiserian style, because he credits Carrie with being an "apt student of fortune's ways" and then adds (after a dash) "of fortune's superficialities" (75), translating what seemed like conscious opportunism into something less imposing yet appropriate for a future Broadway star. He then specifies Carrie's passion for fine clothing as "not fine feeling, it is not wisdom." Equally, however, he adds that "the lowest order of mind is not so disturbed." Nevertheless, fine clothing such as the lace collar speaks to her, "tenderly and Jesuitically for themselves. When she came within earshot of their pleading, desire in her bent a willing ear. The voice of the so-called inanimate! Who shall translate for us the language of the stones?" Might the Biblical echo constitute an apology for Carrie? And her new shoes talk to her of "such little feet," an attribute considered graceful and beautiful by her culture (75). These pathetic fallacies fabricate a modernized pastoral world in which our gentle shepherdess has exchanged her shepherd swain for a traveling salesman, and we find tongues not in the babbling brooks but in the fine clothes of the department store showcases. Carrie is romanticized and made one with her environment. Such paragraphs, often in highly figured and overwrought language, appear at several points in the text.

Two other elements in chapter 11 further advance our understanding of Carrie's qualities. The first is the "educating and wounding" passage in which Drouet, ogling other women even with Carrie on his arm, follows the grace of women: "He had just enough of the feminine love of dress to be a good judge—not of intellect, but of clothes" (76). His remarks to Carrie lead her first to look and observe, then to sense her possible defect, and then "instinctively" to imitate the better style. Finally, as Drouet, worshipper at the shrine of grace that he is, goes on educating and wounding Carrie, she improves herself, for "one of her mind sees many things . . . admired, [and] she gathers the logic of it and applies accordingly" (76). Carrie is a hardworking student of the feminine. She is designated as suffering for her achievements in grace, soon to be recognized by Hurstwood, and she is progressing rapidly to a new state. Thus, although her moral situation deteriorates in conventional terms, her status as a heroine advances; and because she begins earning her future success, we like her. Also, of course, Carrie's advancement limits the Drouet-Carrie union, so a mechanism for the advancement of the plot is established.

Set directly against the blandishments of a superficial world, with which Carrie blends homogeneously and perfectly, is the "ache" of morality. The conscience "called to her in vain" to put on old clothes and old shoes: "She could possibly have conquered the fear of hunger and gone back; the thought of hard work and a narrow round of suffering would, under the last pressure of conscience, have yielded, but spoil her appearance?—be old-clothed and poor-appearing?— never!" (75–76). In an odd reversal of what we would normally expect, her superficial-seeming materialism gives her strength, although not necessarily *moral* strength. In chapter 3 of the Pennsylvania edition a lengthy passage identifies the "drag of desire" as bordering on the poetic and offers a poetics of materialism: "If nothing in the heavens, or the earth, or the waters, could elicit her fancy or delight her from its spiritual or artistic side, think not that the material would be lost" (Penn, 23). The artistry of clothes provides its own impulse of perfect harmony. Poe's angel Israfel could not be more firmly fixed in a scheme of universal harmony than Carrie is in a scheme of material desire. Carrie is actually distinguished by having a slightly different longing than we do. Dreiser gives her heroism with the suggestion that she would accept suffering if she had to, but, in snatching away her ability to resist what comes her way, he confers on her the special qualities that will account for her rise in the theater, her need for appearance, which is the one constant in her otherwise wavering ideologies and allegiances. Consequently, the standards of morality remain an ache rather than a fixed principle of action while Carrie follows a principle that originates in her feminine nature. Whether or not this is sexism on Dreiser's part or on the part of nineteenth-century culture is a moot point, but such treatment appears to make a sexist principle into a grandiose lever of the action.

The second notable element of chapter 11 occurs when Dreiser enhances Carrie, while still limiting her mental promise, by developing a strain of character in her that is sympathetic. Limiting her early tutor Mrs. Hale, a resident of Drouet's boardinghouse, Dreiser tells us that "such conventional expression of morals as sifted through the passive creature's mind, fell upon Carrie and for a while confused her" (77). Portraying Carrie on the one hand as dominated by social beliefs, Dreiser moderates the portrait on the very next line beginning "on the other hand," and speaking of the corrective influence of her own feelings. He leads us to "those things which address the heart," but he leaves ambiguous the value that we are to attach to this characterization. Further, we are told a few paragraphs later that Carrie was affected by music: "Her nervous composition responded to certain strains, much as certain strings of a harp vibrate. . . . She was delicately moulded [*sic*] in sentiment" (77). This flattering description elevates

Carrie nearly to the level of a romantic heroine, and it might be remembered that Poe flattered the angel Israfel by likening his heart-strings to a lute. Carrie is then transported to her "window looking out," wistful, depressed, repentant, and with a wandering mind bringing in the "sheaves of withered and departed joys" (77), a further reminder that a religious revival hymn would have little power in her life. Sensitivity is thus Carrie's keynote and her most ennobling feature. When Dreiser places in her hand a novel by Bertha Clay—for him the standard in lowbrow culture and false sentimentality reduced to bathos, and referred to as such later in the novel—he notes that it is Drouet's and a book that "she did not wholly enjoy" (78). When Drouet enters, in fact, he misses hearing the delicate loneliness in Carrie's voice because he "had not the poetry in him" (78). Relentlessly, Dreiser carries on this strain throughout the chapter, introducing Hurstwood, who sees Carrie's freshness, timidity, and grace, "feelings far superior to Drouet at the first glance." The virtues of the heroine, even while deemed materialistic and defined as naturalistic and somehow more animal instinct than consciousness, have managed to elevate her to an appropriate love object. The mixed description of Carrie has much to do with her presence in the rest of the novel as its emotional center, even when Hurstwood comes to dominate the action.

Crucial to the cohesiveness of the novel is the idea that Carrie's seemingly trivial weakness leads to her growing success in a society that craves what she offers. Even slight word manipulations establish this premise. Moving from a religious resonance to a metaphor of food and appetites, Dreiser transforms her from Drouet's little mortal to the delectable morsel of the patrons of the front row in her first Broadway acting part (53, 326). The devouring world wishes to possess her, no matter how vaguely devilish their intentions may be. As she becomes increasingly attractive, she will come to be the opposite of the increasingly shadowed and cheapened Hurstwood. Her weaknesses lead her to success; Hurstwood's equivalent weaknesses of personality destroy him once he becomes the person drawn to another rather than the one drawing another to him.

A brief intrusion of a more broadly theoretical approach to the novel might be appropriate here. As an allegory the novel reflects the kinds of stories that the culture that produced it reenacts over and over again on the world stage. Following the theoretical lines laid down by Suvir Kaul in a recent analysis of Thomas Gray's "Ode on the Death of a Favourite Cat, Drowned in a Tub of Gold Fishes"—in which the cat, like any female, pays the consequences for reaching after all that glitters, which is not gold—suggests that British imperialism suffers the same condition. Likewise, Carrie may represent a broad principle of American culture—its quest for economic domination of the world; she might be seen as an allegory for American ideals, often wavering and compromised in geopolitical application, and serving a variety of self-interested pressure groups. By abstracting the novel one step beyond a reading of Carrie as a representative American figure, we can see her as a representative of cultural impulses in our political process, a reasonable leap if we assume that literature reflects culture.[1] This extension seems consistent, as well, with Dreiser's somewhat mystical communism.

Carrie is a special fusion of female traits that represents what Dreiser conceives of as the creative spirit. To some extent, she even represents the author himself, including a number of sympathetic traits that the author used in portraying his later heroes. Carrie's femininity is part sexuality—the allure of innocence and freshness—and part her special spiritual quality, which sets her above Drouet and Hurstwood. Although Carrie is portrayed as the opposite of the "pythoness" Julia Hurstwood in most respects, but especially because Carrie lacks Julia's moral strength and outrage, some argument could be made for seeing the two figures in similar terms. Mrs. Hurstwood reveals the unbridled mendacity of her economic position but wishes to rise socially and materially as does Carrie; Carrie's impoverished origins and vulnerability to small economic reverses make her tentative and sympathetic, but she too abandons Hurstwood once he no longer fits into her need to rise materially. Rudyard Kipling, among other writers, would have no trouble envisioning such a pair, like the Colonel's lady and Rosie O'Grady, as "sisters under the skin."

Stephen Crane had described the title character of *Maggie, a Girl of the Streets* (1893) as having "blossomed in a mud-puddle" with options that anticipate Carrie's: go to hell or go to work.[2] In a line or two, Crane assigns Maggie to a stool and machine and the dull and dark life of a factory girl, making her eventual seduction all but inevitable. Dreiser ponderously embroiders a similar reference for Carrie when he describes Hurstwood's fascination with "this lily, which had sucked its waxen beauty and perfume below a depth of waters which he had never penetrated and out of ooze and mould [sic] which he could not understand" (108). Hurstwood's inability to conceptualize Carrie's background establishes the grounds for her emotional superiority. Carrie's sympathy with the "under-world of toil" from which she derives her memories is like her yearning for clothes, "the essence of poetic feeling" (108). Her poetry derives not from high idealism and moral purpose, as in the Horatio Alger novels, but from the cellars and narrow factory windows and blast-furnaces—"Her old father, in his flour-dusted miller's suit"—haunting her at odd moments. Carrie's poetry is the poetry of a materialistic girl who understands what it means to have to work so hard and have so little. Thus, the sociological elements in the novel are folded into the consciousness of the title figure.

With all these elements at work, Dreiser "types" Carrie and rounds out her character. Through Carrie Dreiser raises questions about the well-being and progress of the limited American working class, although in the first few words of the novel we are led to believe that she represents a "middle" class. Out of the potential for her "fall," a concept Dreiser confuses apparently on purpose, comes the drama of her story. Carrie is an unsophisticated and natural mind in a general predicament, for she is confronted by an equivocal and undoing superhuman force, like music, the "roar of life." The city suits Dreiser's purpose, for it offers forces of guile and power that can be embodied in wealth and material objects so that he does not have to personalize them in a villain. Not only Drouet and Hurstwood but also the department store and the gaslit restaurant seduce the poor and the weak.

Dreiser's description of Carrie in animal terms tends to move her problem from the moral to the physical realm. As early as chapter 1, Carrie looks at Drouet with "the instincts of self-protection and coquetry mingling confusedly in her brain" (3). Thus, Dreiser's later depreciations of Carrie's intellect have been fully foreshadowed, and Dreiser fulfills this contract when he proposes that "The unintellectual are not so helpless. Nature has taught the beasts of the field to fly when some unheralded danger threatens. She has put into the small, unwise head of the chipmunk the untutored fear of poisons. . . . The instinct of self-protection, strong in all such natures, was roused but feebly, if at all, by the overtures of Drouet" (49). At the same time he characterizes her as partially protected "like the sheep in its unwisdom, strong in feeling" and then adds a paradoxical biblical reference: "He keepeth his creatures whole" (49). This suggests that the animal images are not intended as totally degrading naturalistic allusions, but neither is Carrie guided by religious principles or religious authority despite the misleading implication.

The worsening moral ramifications of Carrie's affairs are blamed on her circumstances, but the ultimately amoral position of the book derives from the choices she makes of her own volition. Having become Drouet's mistress, the heroine, "looked into her glass and saw a prettier Carrie than she had seen before; she looked into her mind, a mirror prepared of her own and the world's opinions, and saw a worse. Between these two images she wavered, hesitating which to believe" (70). Her psychology exists within her social context. Consistent with Dreiser's use of the sociological metaphor we have a corresponding social psychology in the heroine. Carrie judges herself by the world's opinions, but external documentation of them tells her they are counter to her welfare. To further elaborate this point about Carrie's psychology, we need only move down the same page to the point where Carrie argues, pleads, and excuses herself with her own conscience, which is "not a Drouet": "It was only an average little conscience, a thing which represented the world, her past environment, habit, convention, in a confused way. With it, the voice of the people was truly the voice of God" (70). The interplay of the great and the little that has distinguished Carrie from the wealth of the city is continued in this passage. Once again, blame is shifted from Carrie the person to the conventional popular ideal, with some suggestion that "God" is implicated, although the text carefully makes no such claim. This is yet another of the many marvelous passages in which Dreiser deftly undercuts the character's mind but still allows us to retain our sympathy for her as a victim of forces far beyond her control. The reader becomes attached to her even though she lacks the ability to transcend the forces of her world, for she is its victim, not its manipulator.

Elsewhere, images such as the "deep pit," the "vague shadows," and "the mystic scenery" provided in Minnie's dream establish melodramatic alternatives for the mundane Carrie (61). Such mental images help the blank-minded Carrie become an exciting heroine; her life holds the potential for her dramatic rise to stardom, neither through self-protection nor strength of will, but rather through her "drift" and the effect of her emotional "greatness" on the minds of others. The real complexity of Carrie lies in this opposition: the limited spirit and understanding that follows safe moral conventions and understands the danger of the fall versus the questing soul of the vaguely immoral and unconventional drifter—Carrie. The "essence of poetic feeling" (108) in Carrie is compounded by her wistfulness and her desire for pleasure and social position—all terms applied to her in chapter 15 (107). In these traits, Carrie's spirit is indeed parallel to Theodore Dreiser's, and in this she becomes a heroine the reader can become attached to and empathize with. Even a physical characterization is included: "Experience had not yet taken away that freshness of the spirit which is the charm of the body" in such a way as to clearly imply her physicality (107). Carrie includes all possibilities for interpretation.

Carrie's rise in the theater projects the anomalies of her place in American society even as it appears to be a fulfillment of the American dream. Her success is owing to chance, the American pluck born of necessity, and her experience, blended with her special spiritual power to reflect her world. Despite the cloying falsity of the plot of *Under the Gaslight*, Carrie earns sympathy because she identifies with the emotional loss of the character she plays, being herself an outcast. True, Carrie is a sinner, not a wronged innocent, but Dreiser has taken pains to lighten the reader's perception of evil in Carrie and has, in fact, tended to justify her against the conventional social interpretation of a woman in her situation. When Mrs. Vance actually calls her a "little sinner," as mentioned previously, it is merely a casual reference to Carrie having dropped out of contact; the religious idea has been secularized by the worldly woman of New York society. Since Carrie will strongly emphasize the desire for marriage in her liaison with Drouet and her affair with Hurstwood, Dreiser even builds into his plot her recognition that such a marriage should take place. Meanwhile Dreiser, who is notable for his philosophical intrusions, never once intrudes to discuss whether Carrie's desire for marriage is wrong or right, although he does at times point out her naïveté. Wanting to get married is her reflection of appropriate social behavior.

Carrie's personality is somewhat stronger later in the novel as compared to earlier in the novel, but she is still not wholly without self-delusion. Having been given in Ames "an ideal to contrast men by" (239), "not without great gloom," she begins to look at Hurstwood, who is no longer young, strong, and buoyant, "wholly as a man, and not as a lover or husband" (243). Recognizing her "mistake" in being involved with Hurstwood, she also recalls the force with which she was removed from her former life, although she had been in a precarious position. When Hurstwood gives up looking for a job and settles for staying around the house and looking disheveled, Carrie loses her respect for him, yet she wavers between drifting along with him and being assertive (249). Ultimately their relationship is severed when he falls ill and Carrie is unable to be "good-natured and sympathetic" as she wishes, owing in part to his nature (258). Carrie's weariness and discontent with Hurstwood derive from a combination of her yearning for wealth and his knavishness. The heroine is never completely independent of her needs, and when Hurstwood storms out the door after revealing that their marriage is a fraud, "she thought, at first, with the faintest alarm, of being left without money—not of losing him" (267). Truly, Carrie is driven by the need for survival more than by love, but Carrie has lived without real love from the beginning, when her sister emerges from the throng at the railway station bringing "the change of affectional atmosphere" that represents the "cold reality" of the family life of the poor (8). Carrie's abandonment of Hurstwood is ultimately a coldly economic decision, and it shows her as an unpleasantly self-centered human being, but one whose actions derive from needs unrecognized and unmet by the people surrounding her.

Perhaps it is the absence of familial warmth that makes the larger myth of the star so compelling, for a long-standing maxim is that everybody wants to be the darling of everybody's darling. Carrie's humble beginnings and fictional rise fit the historical myths of Broadway perfectly. She is advanced by her natural beauty, luck, and determination, but she is not free from the sadness of the past even once she has achieved great success. Similar patterns show up frequently as the lot of the "star," not only in our contemporary myths, but also as early as the 1880s. One need only turn to the pages of the July 1886 *Demorest's Monthly Magazine* to find in "The American Drama and Its Typical Stars" such an American icon in "Clara Morris, the Emotional Actress."[3] Clara was an orphan, fled advances from an older man at the age of 12, was identified in the chorus line of a Midwest theater as having talent, and made her way to New York and stardom, carrying with her the pain of physical illness. Parallels to Carrie do not extend so far as to suggest that Clara is an outright source, but Clara's story suggests a generalized ethos into which Carrie fits perfectly as an ideal of popular American culture. At the same time the other problems of a dubious sexual history and the haunting sadness of the great, which run through American star worship from Clara Morris to Marilyn Monroe, do not stand in the way of fame but enhance its mystery. Dreiser had already explained Carrie's situation at the time that she had her first success as Laura: the thought of success "hummed in her ears as the melody of an old song," longing for the better life, but she rather modestly states it as a dream of "sometime" getting a place as a "real" actress (129). This haunting sense of unworthiness and the involvement of hidden personal pain and a troubled personal history enlist our sympathies on the side of the successful star. Carrie, like the real actresses such as Clara Morris and, afterwards, Marilyn Monroe, does not come to happiness through the theater. In chapter 12 while she is still with Drouet and being taught envy of the rich by Mrs. Hale, Dreiser flatly states that Carrie is as happy as she would ever be (87). Her elation after Hurstwood has wooed her in chapter 21 is based on his deceit. The choice of ending chapters between the competing texts of the novel must be seen in light of this early statement in chapter 12; the 1900 text has a happier ending, but Carrie is not to be happy in any case. Her first little flat in Chicago is Carrie's happiest moment.

Whether or not Ames is strengthened as a potential third lover for Carrie, Dreiser has taken the position that the conclusion will be the same. Those who argue that Ames in the 1900 version is too little shown to adequately fulfill his role as a spiritual teacher are convincing. The reader wants one of two things from Dreiser's portrayal of Ames: to know that he is not the answer to Carrie's problem of happiness, but merely a step in her progression, or to believe that Ames may hold the answer to her needs. Dreiser seems willing to allow the reader to entertain either position. The answer, of course, has been given in chapter 12: happiness, unlike wealth, is not necessarily progressive, and therefore it does not necessarily come as a result of Carrie's rise to success.

In chapter 32 in a lengthy passage, Carrie retreats to her rocking chair to brood over her dinner with Ames and the Vances, and we see her with her "little hands folded tightly as she thought" (238). Dreiser, having once again made her into the diminutive seeker, establishes the nature of her pain: "Through a fog of longing and conflicting desires she was beginning to see" (238). He immediately leaps to the highest melodramatic language to invoke hope and pity, sorrow and pain, but he does not further define her longing for the "high life in New York" to which she has been exposed at the same time that she has encountered a man who is better than both Hurstwood and Drouet. Thus, typically, Dreiser serves several ends of the novel. He maintains her smallness and her yearning as pathetic, and he treats her new insight not at all harshly, not ironically, although it might well have been, in the hands of a more moralistic author. Her cry "What difference could it make—what difference could it make?" is the true and appropriately inarticulate expression of a woman who has never been good with words but who feels the desire for a finer artistic life nonetheless.

Nor is the modesty of the yearnings of Carrie's soul a mistake in Dreiser's portrayal of her. Carrie clearly outgrows the men around her not only because her selfish ambition progresses but also because she has endured pain coupled with emotional abuse from these men. Hurstwood relies on Carrie's pliancy when he talks her into leaving Chicago with him. True to her intellectual ability, she convinces herself that she likes him; true to her circumstances, she can see no course but to accompany him to New York. True to her wish to accommodate social requirements, she insists on getting married and thinks she is his wife. The chapters from 33 through 37 most clearly lay out this case. After Hurstwood's bad temper makes Carrie feel gloomy over their reduced budget, she is brought to "gnawing contempt" for him: "Of course, as his own self-respect vanished, it perished for him in Carrie" (260–61). Carrie's growing rejection of Hurstwood is based, as was her liking of him, on his nature, not hers. The situation is made dramatic when he announces that she is not married to him, a revelation so shocking to her that it causes her eyes to bug out, "distend" is the word used, and it also leads to her return to the stage. Hurstwood conjures the image of her leaving him, which is a reversal of her fears of just a few pages before. At the same time, Dreiser gives us our real appraisal of the matured Carrie: "In a flash, he thought he foresaw the result of this thing. Now when the worst of the situation was approaching, she would get on the stage in some cheap way and forsake him. Strangely, he had not conceived well of her mental ability. That was because he did not understand the nature of emotional greatness. He had never learned that a person might be emotionally— instead of intellectually—great. Avery Hall was too far away for him to look back and sharply remember. He had lived with this woman too long" (271–72). Dreiser is according Carrie higher status, through the agency of Hurstwood's not recognizing it, than he has granted her previously. Dreiser, even while denying that Carrie is in any way above the middle average, now endows her with special power, even though he uses negatives to describe it.

Carrie

Carrie's economic success is built into a separation from Hurstwood's evaluation of her. The break away from Hurstwood is sometimes analyzed, both by reviewers of the novel and later scholars, as evidence of Carrie's selfish opportunism. Yet Dreiser excuses "her dawning independence: " 'I could do better than that,' ventured Carrie to herself, in several instances. To do her justice, she was right" (282–83). Carrie assesses the abilities of the "women of alleged abilities" and finds confirmation that she has advanced beyond her previous status. Always before shown as a responder to events, she matures toward a kind of independence that constitutes power, cultivating a part of her being that is stronger than Hurstwood's or Drouet's to begin with.

It also seems that Carrie in some way earns the ingredients for spiritual greatness. Hard work on Carrie's part in the chorus line is within her capability. In chapter 42 we find one of the most profound endorsements of Carrie, raising her far above the fate ascribed to a common Sister Emma type. Specifically, at the same time that we learn that Hurstwood is beginning to suffer delusions of his former life in the face of his failure, and as Lola Osborne, "seeing [Carrie] succeeding, had become a sort of satellite" (315), Carrie is thus described: "Timid as Carrie was, she was strong in capability. The reliance of others made her feel as if she must, and when she must she dared. Experience of the world and of necessity was in her favour. . . . She had learned that men could change and fail. . . . It required superiority—kindly superiority—to move her—the superiority of a genius like Ames" (315). Carrie has thus not only risen in economic fortune, having successfully gained a line in a Broadway play and thus emerged from the anonymity of the chorus, but has also emerged spiritually on a higher level. She is credited with leadership, wisdom, and an ability to respond to the best the world offers.

Carrie succeeds because she has emotional—but not intellectual—greatness. Even in summary, Dreiser repeats that it was "by force of her moods alone" that Carrie approached "Chicago, New York; Drouet, Hurstwood; the world of fashion and the world of stage" (368). It is Carrie, not Hurstwood, who is finally lectured in the abstract by the forces of social convention. She is still not free; the specter of Hurstwood haunts her as well as the lowness of her past condition. She is Moll Flanders with a conscience and a burden. Even in the paragraph in which we learn that Drouet has given up on pursuing Carrie and that Hurstwood's body is being freighted to Potter's Field Dreiser claims, "Their influence upon her life is explicable alone by the nature of her longings" (369). The novel is Carrie's to the end, but Dreiser was able to accord her a measure of worldly success at least in part because she is so passive. Because success comes to her and is not a product of her personal force, it does not jeopardize the book's prevailing melancholy message. Chapter 44 shows Carrie as "lonely" from success, from the nonutility of her money, and from the limitations of her knowledge (334–35). From this derives "grieving," "inactivity and longing" (357) in the face of larger challenges of intellection from Ames for which she is not equipped. It may be that as Dreiser brings on the lure of the intellectual, Carrie's tragedy is even deepening in a realm where she has never been competent. Her rocking chair remains for her the place from which she can view and long for the acceptance of the society that created her, a society whose ultimate expectations she can never fulfill and a society that can never bring her the happiness for which she yearns.

9

Four Lovers

The drama of *Sister Carrie* is constructed around all four lovers—Drouet, Carrie, Hurstwood, and Ames—as much as around a single title figure. The triumvirate of Drouet, Carrie, and Hurstwood is the most important aspect of the book, for they compose a single conglomerate striving, to which all of Dreiser's social moralizing contributes. The seduction scene that enfolds Carrie and Drouet at the outset of the novel may seem trivial compared to the larger forces depicted early in the novel, but it is crucial in establishing the foundation for Carrie's later relationships, and it is momentous in philosophical terms for the chief participants. Clearly a localized experience, Drouet's approach to Carrie embodies her superficiality. Hurstwood's fall is pure tragedy, particularly when coupled with Carrie's rise, for Carrie does not really find happiness and therefore *Sister Carrie* can hardly be called a comedy or even a novel of success. Instead, Hurstwood's suffering is internalized within the reader's understanding of Carrie's longing and her poignant yearning after some higher form of happiness. Hurstwood's fall and death—characterized by the image of the boat with its unnamed body crossing the river of death—is so intertwined with Carrie's fame and reclusiveness that the one invests the other with its gloom. This transference of Hurstwood's gloom to Carrie's brilliance is one of the novel's greatest achievements. Ames, although he might be treated as a qualitative advance over Hurstwood and Drouet, is an advance only in intellect, not in significance for the heroine's fulfillment. He is detached from social urges in a way that she can never be. When he harangues Carrie late in the novel, he also "was so interested in forwarding all good causes . . . giving vent to these preachments" that he "wants to stir her up" (357). This language does not identify a man any more interested in Carrie as a person than were Drouet and Hurstwood, who were mostly interested in her as an externalization of their own sexual drives.

DROUET

In representing the superficiality in Carrie's personality yet falling well below the potential of other sides of her personality, Drouet is an appropriate component of the combined personality of the four characters seeking to rise to one ideal state of bliss. In his original characterization of Drouet, Dreiser committed the indiscretion of plagiarizing directly from George Ade's "The Fable of the Two Violin Players and the Willing Performer" from *Fables in Slang*. Dreiser's indifference to building up Drouet's portrait by this borrowing suggests his intention for Drouet's role, for the salesman demonstrates shallowness and a kind of self-serving egoism. Starting from Ade's description, Dreiser expands Drouet into a stronger figure, but he always subordinates Drouet to the more forceful figures around him, ultimately including the maturing Carrie, at the end of the novel.

As a borrowing from Ade, Drouet is a representative figure of his period. In Ade's fable, however, the "willing performer" courts and marries for money, displacing a less aggressive pair of "Conventional Young Men." Ade thus presented his conventional but not necessarily sophisticated readers with a satire on themselves, played against the more successfully rude, unconventional suitor. Ade's representation of the masher as one who approaches women boldly was elaborated more imaginatively by Dreiser. As Ellen Moers has pointed out in *Two Dreisers*, Drouet is the summer alternative to the surrounding chill of wintry circumstances that are driving Carrie into sickness and despair. Moers, noting the use of the word "radiance" repeatedly in descriptions of Drouet, writes, "Warmth emanates from Drouet, who, . . . is 'rosy cheeked,' 'the essence of sunshine,' and to whom Carrie is the 'daisy' of the fields. His 'geniality' and 'exuberance' are the sun that 'warms her heart' " (Moers 1969, 149). Moers documents the contrast between Drouet's vegetable warmth and the increasing speed of the Hurstwood seduction and the cold of New York City. She sees Dreiser's sense of a positive component in Drouet, despite his shallowness. Dreiser borrowed Ade's representation because he saw Drouet essentially as a flat character rather than a developed villain; he develops him as a muted comic alternative in his own more substantive way.

Drouet is neither a model hero nor a villain. Almost from the first Drouet is a foil for higher natures. In allowing Carrie to formulate "a true estimate of Drouet" in chapter 7, Dreiser makes clear that he is not evil, but "he was a creature of inborn desire" with "no mental process in him worthy the dignity" of terms like "speculation" or "philosophising" (48). Dreiser is at pains, in fact, to identify Drouet's own vulnerability with the worst aspects of Carrie's status—although in good clothes and health he is a "merry, unthinking moth of the lamp," he would be as helpless and pitiable as Carrie if he were "struck by a few of the involved and baffling forces which sometimes play upon man" (48). Drouet, as the subject of Dreiser's analysis of men's pursuit of women, "meant them no harm" but merely loved to make advances and have women succumb "because his inborn desire urged him to that as a chief delight" (49). This avocation parallels Carrie's love of beautiful things, but there are real social dangers for the victims of his conquests that called on Dreiser's contemporary readers to reject him. So Dreiser differentiates him from a true villain by portraying him as capable of being as easily "hornswaggled" by a true villain as he himself flattered a pretty girl. He could, in fact, be "as deluded by fine clothes as any silly-headed girl" (49). Such egregious sexism is not merely gratuitous on Dreiser's part, for it allies Drouet with Carrie and helps justify Carrie's compromise of her virtue by accepting $20 from Drouet: "The best proof that there was something open and commendable about the man was the fact that Carrie took the money" (49). Of necessity, particularly in light of the deeper naturalist philosophical passages about life that appear in the first portion of the book, Carrie and Drouet share in a certain superficial naïveté.

Dreiser soon turns to showing us Drouet's spiritual deficiencies in relation to Hurstwood and to Carrie, even though, like her, when he reappears at the end of the novel, somewhat unexpectedly, he has risen economically. Drouet's deficiencies, like his charity toward pretty young girls, are superficialities of his nature and social status. We are still in chapter 7 when Dreiser writes that "Carrie had more imagination than he—more taste" (53). Also, Dreiser places Drouet in the same self-befuddled moral state as Carrie, for when Drouet says he will help her find a job—by implication instead of supporting her as a mistress—"He really imagined that he would" (55). Later on, however, as Hurstwood emerges, Drouet is lowered in Carrie's estimation. First, he is "slightly inconsiderate" and shows himself "not to have the keenest sensibilities" (71). She is "more clever than" he, and soon she "dimly" begins to "see where he lacked" refinement (72). With Hurstwood set up in opposition—his understated evening coat versus Drouet's bright plaid, and the dull shine of his leather shoes to Drouet's glassy patent leather—Drouet is obviously a grade inferior to this other protagonist. "Not tactful," in manners as in clothes, is how Dreiser describes Drouet in chapter 11, "educating and wounding" (76) Carrie by pointing out to her the graces of other women—which she, in her turn, will emulate. Carrie becomes more refined at the same time that she begins to judge Drouet. Drouet is oblivious to others' feelings except in a superficial way that perfectly accompanies his dress as a "masher." Yet, he is kindly disposed toward Carrie, and he does extend help to her out of a generalized kindliness motivated by a sexual spring of which he is not fully aware. And his liaison with her does provide her with the opportunity to elevate her own fortunes to the extent that she can attract a man like Hurstwood. Critical though we are expected to be of Drouet, his plaint that Carrie "didn't do me right" is not completely without its poignance when their affair is terminated. Similarly, his charity to the poor allows us to relate Drouet, as we related Carrie in the previous chapter, to a cultural allegory, or at least to a paradigm of American cultural behavior that maintains its charitable side even though its primary pursuit is not the well-being of others as much as "variable pleasure."

As Carrie improves under Drouet's unaware tutelage, Hurstwood is identified as Drouet's rival for the first time in chapter 11 and knows that he feels "contempt" for the drummer: Drouet "had no power of analyzing the glance and the atmosphere of a man like Hurstwood" (81). Dreiser shows Drouet to be no more perceptive in sizing up Hurstwood as a rival than he is at analyzing Carrie as a lover. A review of the scale of images Dreiser applies to Drouet is helpful here. Even as Dreiser first defined Drouet's personality in Carrie's eyes in chapter 7, he animalizes him, just before referring to Carrie's chipmunk-brained self-protective instinct, he equally demeans Drouet: "A Madame Sappho would have called him a pig" (49). Dreiser adds, as if working down a scale, Shakespeare would have called him a "merry child," his boss a "clever, successful business man," and he himself "as good as his intellect conceived" (49). A repulsive animal to any self-aware woman, Drouet is still a hero within his limitations. As such, he is like Carrie, for she will also rise to the ultimate level of her limitations, as Dreiser will repeat even as he raises her limitations during the course of the novel. Both characters rise from the simpler animal to the more complex spiritual limits of their intellects, more united than antagonistic, even as Carrie pulls away from Drouet's lower nature.

As compared to Hurstwood's view of Drouet, Carrie sees him as "a kindly soul, but otherwise defective" (83). Adverbs like "foolishly" begin to be attached to Drouet's actions as they will later fall on Hurstwood's; Drouet is so described twice (76, 83), and Hurstwood will later gain the same term at least once (161). As Hurstwood's seduction continues, Carrie is moved by "secret current feelings which Drouet had never understood" (88). This masterpiece of awkward phraseology nonetheless indicates the standing of the two lovers in relation to Carrie's erotic impulses.

Despite his cataloging of all of Drouet's spiritual limitations,

Dreiser is careful to maintain a sense of his basic charitable nature, possibly because Drouet in an alternate role would be merely a vile seducer. To maintain a sense of Carrie as somehow better than a fallen woman for his readers of 1900, Dreiser must create some sympathy for Drouet. Critics have rightly drawn attention to a moment at the end of chapter 14 when Drouet, Hurstwood, and Carrie exit from the play "The Covenant." Drouet, this time through action rather than through reflective commentary, is shown to be insensitive when he criticizes the play's cuckolded husband, who has been inattentive to his wife, and whose role Drouet is unwittingly living: "served him right, I haven't any pity for a man who would be such a chump as that." At that moment, at Hurstwood's side, a beggar asks for money: Drouet hands the man a dime; Hurstwood "scarcely noticed"; and Carrie "quickly forgot" (103). Drouet is portrayed as the most sympathetic character towards the poor. His shallowness and his strengths are commingled. At the end of the novel when he reappears and hopes to reestablish his relationship with Carrie on the same old basis, and even comments more or less indifferently on Hurstwood's theft, he retains much the same characteristics; although more prosperous and somewhat heavier of girth, he is neither deeper in understanding nor shallower in sympathy.

Carrie's rise through the theater and break with Drouet shows no further development of his character. Although Drouet is far more rounded than any "flat" or stock figure, his "type" limits his personality and drags on hers. During the dramatic production, Drouet is important in bolstering Carrie's spirit, but after she gains her success, in sentence after sentence, Hurstwood is mentioned first and Drouet afterwards, a pale imitation, but yet self-deluded: "Drouet hung on, thinking he was all in all. The dinner was spoiled by his enthusiasm" (141). Even in the climactic chapter 23 where Carrie and Drouet argue over rights and responsibilities, Drouet's egotism prevents him from insight. He enters unable to read her, the half-light of the room conceals her blushes, and even though Carrie answers his charges out of a "confused little brain," Drouet, "irritated but fascinated" can only be amazed and hurt at Carrie's seeming disloyalty (163–65). Drouet's statement, ultimately delivered twice, that Cad did not "do me right" lacks force to the reader because he had not done her right in seducing her and falsely promising to marry her, which would have made her an honest women. On the other hand, Drouet makes a fairly reasonable complaint, if we disallow the problem of sin/marriage—as Dreiser partly wishes us to do—and regard Drouet as a merry good fellow willing to help another person along. Nonetheless, when Carrie declares to Drouet, "Whatever has happened is your own fault," she speaks the truth (169).

Drouet, for all his characteristics is a brilliant embodiment of the kind of limited mind that he, Carrie, and others share, and those with such minds survive when more forceful natures might fail. Carrie's emotional greatness will bring her further on the stage, but Drouet embodies Carrie's superficiality in the early progress of the novel, and Dreiser uses him at the end of the novel to measure the potential for change in a feeling character like Carrie. His experience represents what Dreiser wishes us to understand is one of many potentials surrounding Carrie. At the end of the novel, in chapter 46, Drouet reenters much as he was. Still a "genial egotist" (350), "handsome as ever, after his kind," he leaves the "bright" dinner table with reluctance, not being able to "restore their old friendship at once and without modification" (349) even though he is "but slightly changed" (348). Drouet represents the limitations of the truly superficial. Dreiser frees Carrie and makes her superior to these limitations, leaving Drouet as their representative, but he is also a figure who can, metaphorically, float above the misfortunes that overwhelm Hurstwood. The last line devoted to him describes his "creaking off in his good shoes" to the elevator: "The old butterfly was as light on the wing as ever" (364).

HURSTWOOD

Hurstwood is the third crucial member of the initial triumvirate of Chicago seekers who occupy our attention. It is because of Hurstwood's failure and a drive of even stronger necessity than that which caused her union with Drouet that Carrie reaches for greater potential. Hurstwood has often been seen as stealing Carrie's novel, both by early reviewers and later critics, but a good case can be made for his being an appropriate component of the joint personality comprised of all four romantic figures. Together they represent the stuggle to overcome limitations on the human will, and its commitment to yearning. To see them as more independent than this, in fact, dictates a plot structure much closer to that forthcoming with *The Financier*, published a decade later. Hurstwood has some of the drive that Drouet lacks, and he is a more predatory and a stronger figure, but his powers are equally limited. His responsiveness to Carrie is an evolutionary advance over Drouet; he represents a progression in Carrie's desire for the good things of life, but his attraction to her is also a weakness that brings about his downfall. His defeat is a tragedy that lends a sense of hollowness and defeat to Carrie's success. Early in the novel, however, the language of defeat foreshadowing Hurstwood's end is attached to Drouet, who carries "the doom of all enduring relationships" in his unstable superficiality, and who will remain so young in spirit "until he was dead" (93). At this point, Hurstwood is designated as "alive" and "a youth again," but by the end of the novel, the word "doom" will have shifted to him, since it was he who was willing to sell his soul for the Paradise of Carrie (141,151).

Hurstwood gets into trouble only by willfully changing from his circumspect character (66) and "forget[ing] the need of circumspectness" (140), and finally, harassed by thoughts of his love, he comes to a passion no longer colored by reason (150). Even late in the novel, his pride leads him at several points, just as his lust and drinking led him to take the money from the safe. Personal characteristics seem central, but they are not controlling. Both Carrie and Hurstwood are sincere, but they are weak. William James argues in *Psychology: The Briefer Course* that the formation of the "self" comes from competing "Me's"—a social Me, a religious Me, a materialist Me, and so on. James uses such terms as "social self-seeking" in ways reflected in Dreiser's portrait of Carrie, Bertil Nelson has argued, and explains the spiritual self's importance in human life, and as Dreiser portrays it in

Carrie's aspirations.[1] In Jamesian terms, Hurstwood undergoes a radical shift in commitment from the social Me, represented so patently in all members of the Hurstwood household, to a materialist Me that determines his ethical choices and defines his character (Nelson, 52, 61). As Nelson points out, the locking of the safe, for example, was ethically neutral, but the choice not to return the money was a conscious future-shaping decision. Ultimately, then, Hurstwood is responsible for himself and his self, equally. When he reaches New York and recognizes his diminished status his life becomes a stunning illustration of the consequences foreseen by William James's psychological theories: "There are few men who would not feel personally annihilated if a life-long construction of their hands or brains, . . . were suddenly swept away . . . a sense of the shrinkage of our personality, a partial conversion of ourselves to nothingness, which is a psychological phenomenon by itself" (Nelson 59). Hurstwood is both a creator and a creation of his desire, and in this he is true to the analytic model James puts forth and that Dreiser seems to have employed.

As Donald Pizer has noted, Hurstwood is portrayed as an impressive figure in his world but is really the "butt of semi-comic irony" in his inability to control his own home and wife (Pizer, 80). Hurstwood's clothing, his manners, his influence among his peers, who are "many and influential," is as subtle as Cowperwood's in *The Financier* in larger circumstances, and he has the power, initially, to rally them "like Romans to a senator's call" (127). Such forceful imagery easily elevates him above Drouet and explains why his interest in Carrie could cause her to begin "dwelling on the atmosphere which this man created for her" (148). Nor does it seem illogical in chapter 21 that Carrie finds him a man who can "delude her into the belief that she was possessed of a lively passion for him" (149). "Not grieved" by Hurstwood's love, she languishes affectionately on "a borderless sea of speculation" particularly confused by her inability to determine if Drouet would marry her or if he considered her his wife—because Dreiser wants to show us that Carrie's drift in moral issues is determined by conventional ideas developing in response to the characters of the men who pursue her. In chapter 21 Carrie turns on Hurstwood the implications of his own passionate urgings and asks when they will be married. For Carrie this is a sincere question, even as it shows us the relatively subordinated nature of both her passion and her morality to the social need of reputation—a need plainly evidenced on a stuffier level by the already existing Hurstwood family. She and they are, finally, the same in their sense of a need for social acceptability.

In part because of the foregoing, Donald Pizer's discussion of Hurstwood sees him as essentially weak, leading a "moral life of indecision and accident rather than of purposeful drift" (Pizer, 73), but the description of Hurstwood in relation to the other lovers also leaves him less of a failure spiritually. As Pizer argues convincingly, Hurstwood fails to realize that his power is only that of appearance, but Dreiser may not see this as wholly unnatural, and Hurstwood's social situation is still a step above Drouet's and the original Carrie's. In other words, as Pizer suggests, Hurstwood is a step up on the same ladder, but he also holds an array of skills that he can marshal successfully. In reflecting the power of longing for youth and beauty, he expresses, in fact, a vital component of the artist Dreiser—who would later gain a reputation as a womanizer—and of Carrie herself. Dreiser plainly labels all of Hurstwood's manifestations as a lover from the outset as being components of a youth that Hurstwood no longer possesses. Yet his passion for Carrie, brought forth by her appeal as a yearning figure, is a response to her finest, not her worst, traits—her own freshness, beauty, and longing, materialistic though it may be seen in most parts of the novel. In Hurstwood's responsiveness, then, something good and heroic is nascent, despite our critical rejection of him.

It is as a rival of Drouet that Hurstwood appears at his best, but his best is deceptive for us as readers because it makes him appear more decisive than the sociological trap of New York will allow him to be. By the end of chapter 11, Carrie has shifted allegiance, finding Hurstwood a superior man: "She instinctively felt that he was stronger and higher . . . that Drouet was only a kindly soul, but otherwise defective" (82–83). Drouet is seen as "foolishly" idling away his romantic prospects. For Carrie, the conflict leaves her rocking "sad beyond measure, and yet uncertain, wishing, fancying," hardly the response of a worldly jezebel (87). Drouet's "good-natured egotism" cannot see "something delicate and lonely" in Carrie (78); whereas Hurstwood "gave her credit for feelings superior to Drouet at the first glance" (79). His eye gains the gleam of a rival, he is a spider spinning gossamer web, and "he began to look to see where he was weak," finally examining Drouet "with the eye of a hawk" (80–81). Sympathy and selfishness mingle in Hurstwood and lead him to court Carrie; he is described as literally glowing "with his own intensity, and the heat of his passion was already melting the wax of his companion's scruples" (96). The force of the imagery is not without its heroic overtones. In the same paragraph, Carrie abandons her attempts to formulate any "thought which would be just and right" and accepts the warmth. Hurstwood is a powerful wooer; yet Carrie is hardly devoted to him in the way a true lover should be. The highest that can be said of Carrie's attraction to Hurstwood is probably Dreiser's representation a few pages later in chapter 14 that he "seemed a drag in the direction of honour," the glimmering of a way out of her unmarried status with the light-footed Drouet (98), much as he will later seem a "drag on her soul," after he lurches out of her life for the last time into the wintry New York night (352).

Hurstwood's force as a person is undermined quickly as he is shown realizing the complications of Carrie's wooing but only deferring his strategy in minor ways. While Drouet treats her "claims upon his justice" airily, Hurstwood actually takes on the role of deceiver, although it is Carrie who is doing the deceiving. The seeds of Hurstwood's own spiritual rise are planted here, nonetheless, for he, not lowering himself to ridicule Drouet, "felt the injustice of the game as it stood, and was not cheap enough to add to it the slightest mental taunt" (103). Still, he allows Carrie to delude herself that he will marry her—the very element that will finally prompt her to leave him in New York in his decline. Thus, there is much in this interplay to suggest that Hurstwood has a weakness as fatal as Drouet's—his inability to face the final issue for Carrie of becoming a married woman. This failure will later be compounded when he falsely ascribes to her the limitations of a "thoroughly domestic type" only because he has himself limited her to life away from the "shine and glow of life" and begins to ignore her so much that she begins to sense the difference (214–15).

Hurstwood's tragic fall will derive from his blindness to social limitations and his sense of honor. It is indeed a classical Greek tragedy in which he names his own vice and pursues it until it destroys him. In Hurstwood's case, the machinery is established clearly in chapter 9. Having no more than temporary dissatisfaction with his own wife, he counterbalances an occasional lusty thought with "his social position and a certain matter of policy" (66). Circumspectness is his guiding law; conventional things protect against the "scandal" that might get him into trouble—thus Dreiser's words are purposefully mundane. Carrie and Drouet's domestic arrangement corresponds to this caution except at a lower rung on the social ladder. The paradigm for the manager's own fate is provided in his view of middle-class individuals who get into trouble: "If it came up for discussion among such friends as with him passed for close, he would deprecate the folly of the thing. 'It was all right to do it—all men do those things—but why wasn't he careful? A man can't be too careful.' He lost sympathy for the man that made a mistake and was found out" (66–67). It will be characteristic from the moment that Hurstwood meets Carrie that he begins to be less than normally careful. He leans too far forward in the theater box with Drouet and Carrie so that his son sees him, and ultimately he takes the money after moving it from the safe at Fitzgerald and Moy's. From the train-ride out of Chicago what the reader experiences on Hurstwood's behalf are the consequences of his social fall, the terrible and irrevocable retribution.

So it is in chapter 19 that Hurstwood "forgot the need of circumspectness which his married state enforced" (140), and in chapter 21 he comes to feel "an elation which was tragic in itself" (148). Remarkably early in the novel he is "a vessel, powerful and dangerous, but rolling and floundering without sail" (160). Thus it is that the word "scandal" falls on Hurstwood in chapter 27 of the novel's 47 chapters (193). His exiting comment with his satchel of purloined money is his own epitaph: "I wish I hadn't done that. . . . That was a mistake" (194). The definition of a fall in Hurstwood's own terms is thus what convicts him for the reader—a fall from his social rather than his moral position. His on-going tragedy derives from his breaking his own law of life as well as breaking manmade law: " 'What a fool I was to do that,' he said over and over. 'What a mistake!' . . . In his sober sense, he could scarcely realize that the thing had been done. He could not begin to feel that he was a fugitive from justice. He had often read of such things, and had thought they must be terrible, but now that the thing was upon him, he only sat and looked into the past. . . . He surveyed his actions for the evening, and counted them parts of a great mistake" (197). The word "mistake" (67), Hurstwood's own key to condemnation, is the word that haunts him even before he has completed his flight. Following in chapter 28 comes an even lengthier consideration of his "own error" in which he wishes to return to his "dignity, his merry meetings, his pleasant evenings" (202). In short, the tragedy of Hurstwood is played out as if he were indeed the Roman senator to whom his friends rallied earlier in the novel (127), but now he is betrayed by his fall from his own standards of moral action—circumspection and caution. Dreiser later expanded this motivation in Frank Cowperwood in *The Financier*; here it is rudimentary in its development.

Carrie's responses to Hurstwood reflect Hurstwood's turmoil. Already seeing himself as an embezzler "known for what he was," he projects something into Carrie in Canada which "forbade" him embracing her: "His opinion was the result of his own experiences and reflections below stairs" (207). Dreiser, for the second time, attaches the idea of tragedy to Hurstwood—his defalcation "a single point in a long tragedy"—which effects him with a "deep gloom" and moral revulsion (219, 242–43). This will ultimately color all his relations with Carrie. "Gloom" will come to be the predominant note of their flat as an outcome of the one wavering moment when he sacrifices "all that he most respected on this earth"; he takes on the role of the fallen outcast that has for so long threatened Carrie.

Later in the novel when Hurstwood carefully leaves exact change on the kitchen table we see the alternative tragic rise of Hurstwood measured in pennies. When Hurstwood originally entered into the theft of money from the safe, Dreiser took pains to note that Hurstwood was oblivious to the "true ethics of the situation . . . under any circumstances" (193). In chapter 39 Hurstwood returns "accurate" change for a half dollar, according to Dreiser's arithmetic (28 + 32 = 50), causing Carrie to conclude that all he wanted of her was something to eat: "He had no vices" (285). With Hurstwood's doom closely pursuing him, we are given to understand that his rectitude is now higher, in a way, than it appeared earlier in the novel, and he continues in this mode even as the ultimate destroying power of "drift" closes in on him. Indeed, Hurstwood's whole attitude of letting Carrie have her fame without troubling her is an expansion of this tragic principle, expressed in "almost inexplicable apathy" as Carrie and opportunity both drift out of his life (289). Even to the very last, having a quarter instead of the 15¢ needed for a flophouse suicide causes him to go on—although Dreiser states it as the idea passing out of his mind, so far gone is his humanity and his control of his own thinking: "It was only when he could get nothing but insults that death seemed worth while" (361).

In conjunction with plot imagery, the imagery of Hurstwood's fall is one of the most stunning aspects of the second half of the novel, placing him spiritually at the center of our consciousness. Not only does the imagery foreshadow Hurstwood's suicide; it also follows him into the Danteian inferno represented by the Broadway firesigns— consistent with the imagery of the 1870s popular press as cited earlier—but that also symbolize Carrie's rise to stardom and success, a bitter irony. From the reader's viewpoint, Hurstwood's plight may derive from Carrie's earlier difficulties. Even in the first chapters of the novel, the imagery and language of the hellish Broadway firesigns and the doom of Hurstwood were prefigured in Carrie's life, for in chapter 4 Dreiser notes of Carrie's subdued spirits, "Only the ashes of all her fine fancies were remaining—ashes still concealing, nevertheless, a few red embers of hope" (26). He continues later on the same page to note how sunshine reassures her, for "out in the sunlight there is, for a time, cessation even of the terror of death" (26). Appropriately, these crucial images lead directly to Carrie going forth into Chicago's Fifth Avenue—a walled canyon of brownstone—where the weak-kneed heroine embodies her fears, without directly expressing them: "She wondered at the magnitude of this life and at the importance of knowing much in order to do anything in it at all. Dread at her own inefficiency crept upon her. She would not know how, she would not be quick enough" (26). This paragraph defines Carrie but also defines the great problem of the novel and explains why Carrie at the end of the novel is still a sympathetic figure who seems to have come full circle; Hurstwood now has the reality of an economic fall from grace as *his* punishment. The Algeresque desire to be a good competitor— or rather the fear of not being one or knowing how to be one—is transferred from the definition of Carrie's character to the actuality of Hurstwood's decline through the events of the plot; he will live out her worst terrors, only "stealing" the novel from her insomuch as the characters are perceived independently. The darkness of the Hanson flat and the factory do not leave the novel, for the alleys off Broadway convey the same sense of darkness made more lurid rather than lightened. The foreshadowing leads from a limited worldview to ultimate doom. At least the reader's emotional experience of the world supersedes an individual's well-being, the point on which much of the philosophy of the book seems to hang.

The decline in the fortunes of Carrie and Hurstwood as lovers corresponds to Hurstwood's socioeconomic decline, and the waning of love in the pair is the inevitable result of their circumstances rather than their sins. We had been told that she had no great passion for Hurstwood (211). Passive and reactive as Carrie is, Hurstwood's neglect of her naturally breaches their relationship, understandably enough, since Carrie had only had a delusion of love anyway (150–51, 221). With Hurstwood's decline, however, "the delight of love had again slipped away," banishing the last trace of youth and thrusting Carrie gradually first into aloofness, then avoidance, and finally into action. Much of the burden of chapter 34 is to show how Hurstwood and Carrie exchange roles, with their relationship being the casualty of the reversal. Ames is designated as better than both of Carrie's previous lovers at the outset.

Shortly after Carrie meets Ames and is introduced to the "high life in New York" we begin encountering the imagery of Hurstwood's decline. The text has warned us that "katastates" will break down a man's body and that gloomy drifting now characterizes the life of Carrie and Hurstwood together; however, much of the imagery is even more foreboding than this. Hurstwood says to Carrie, in regard to his loss of the New York saloon venture, "Well . . . to-day's my last day on earth" (250). Since walking and physical exercise are not easy to such a portly gentleman of the advanced age of 43, however, he soon buries himself in the "Lethian waters" of the newspapers (252).[2] Although it was long before, we might well remember that after Carrie's first theatrical, Hurstwood "could have sold his soul to be with her alone" (141). After further pages detailing Hurstwood's decline through gambling, Dreiser further advises us "Like a morphine fiend, he was becoming addicted to his ease" (267). The metaphor of decline thus increases from chair warmer to dope addict. Treating himself to a hotel dinner, he enters a period of "self-forgetfulness" as if "lured by a phantom" (268). Death images characterize Hurstwood when Carrie ventures to try her luck with theater managers at the end of chapter 37, and Hurstwood is "dead to the horror of it" (276); like Carrie in times of reflection, he merely continues to rock to and fro. His further attempts to evade his destiny are futile, for when Hurstwood juggles grocery bills to stave off payment, and "The game of a desperate man had begun" (288) in economic terms, he is already dead in metaphor. By chapter 42, the room is "ghostlike" as Hurstwood remembers older conversations (315), and, finally, as Carrie makes up her mind to leave in the same chapter, Hurstwood rocks and reads on in his newspaper, "All unconscious of his doom" (318). Practically speaking, the book ends with this chapter, when Hurstwood, rocking and pitying himself in the abandoned flat says out loud, as if expressing his own epitaph, "I tried, didn't I?" (321).

Finally, the contrast in Carrie's and Hurstwood's fate is expressed through the imagery of heaven and hell. Carrie has reached heaven at the end of chapter 43, where Hurstwood, brooding in a third-rate hotel on Bleecker Street, recognizes her luck in terms of the "walled city" of plush covers, lights, and ornaments: "Ah, she was in the walled city now! Its splendid gates had opened, admitting her from a cold, dreary outside. She seemed a creature afar off—like every other celebrity he had known" (328). The little pilgrim has succeeded in her quest for business success. In contradistinction to the heavenly images surrounding Carrie, Hurstwood becomes an "apparition" (352) to Carrie; he "shifted by curious means" and "toward the dead of winter" is unaware of Carrie's return to Broadway (353). Lurid hellfire is suggested as "for weeks he wandered about the city, begging, while the firesign, announcing her engagement, blazed nightly upon the crowded street of amusements" (353). The device both announces her success and symbolizes his on-coming fate. Finally consigned to his peculiarly Danteian sociological circle, Hurstwood becomes merely one of many homeless, "pale, flabby, sunken-eyed, hollow-chested, with eyes that glinted and shone and lips that were a sickly red by contrast. . . . They were of the class which simply floats and drifts, every wave of people washing up one, as breakers do driftwood upon a stormy shore" (358). Thus, for all the discussion of Dreiser's philosophy, it is also with the classic devices of the novel that his power rests—metaphor and the socialized and urbanized imagery of the naturalist's vision, translated here into visions of heaven and hell. Carrie's involvement with these devices, such as the firesigns, and her frequently restated loneliness, connects her to the atmosphere surrounding Hurstwood long after their close ties have been severed. Hurstwood's adoption of her rocking chair and his walk in the lurid light of the firesigns is her doom also.

AMES

Ames, succeeding Hurstwood as Carrie's potential lover, is often considered the solution to Carrie's yearning for a richer, fuller life. He is modeled, as students of Dreiser sources have ably shown, on inventor Elmer Gates, with more than passing touches of Thomas Alva Edison thrown in.[3] As Hurstwood is used as a foil to show off Drouet's failings, so Ames appears to be a step beyond Hurstwood. Ames is a midwestern inventor whose successful inquiries into electrical inventions occur in the background of the novel. His impact on Carrie is intellectual, for he is the agent for the development of a new and enlarged circle of yearnings in her soul. Notably, when Carrie and Ames are first introduced in chapter 32, where Ames is described as a "courageous" midwesterner of free ideas, Carrie's past is brought particularly to the forefront to contrast with the "showy, unwholesome, and wasteful" eating habits of Americans, surrounded by gestures and trappings bought by money: "the other Carrie—poor, hungry, drifting" (234) is resurrected, giving Carrie the first of many sad moments developing out of their acquaintanceship. Dreiser establishes a platform in Carrie's feelings for Ames, who, a page later, profiled with the high forehead and wide mouth of an Edison, remarks that it is "a shame for people to spend so much money this way" (235). When Carrie feels that Ames is "thinking about something over which she had never pondered," and later other "strange things," the novelist is actually engaging in authorial misdirection, for we know that Carrie has just been having very strong feelings about these matters, based on her own experience. Ames also attacks modern literature, including *Dora Thorne*, and Carrie looks at him, "as to an oracle" (236–37). Ames is not sarcastic, although he brings Carrie the "pain of not understanding." We are told, "This man was far ahead of her. He seemed wiser than Hurstwood, saner and brighter than Drouet" (237). Notably, however, even here she realizes that "his interest in her was a far-off one." Ames does endorse the theater, at least, although the general run of his conversation sets Carrie again "rocking, and beginning to see" (238), but the intellectual approach to life that is Ames's heroic quality—the quality of Edisonian invention—holds no promise as a satisfaction or resolution for her. His "calm indifference" to social contrasts is without sensuality; thus he represents in a character the distanced philosophical position of Epictetus "who smile[s] when the last vestige of physical welfare is removed" (241), a distance Hurstwood cannot reach as he sees the walled city from outside (241). Ames, unlike Hurstwood, is undergoing no deprivation.

As Carrie gains a position in the chorus of a Broadway show, we are actually introduced to the *meaning* of the lovers Hurstwood and Ames, expanding on the statement in chapter 34 that Ames is "stronger and better" than Hurstwood and Drouet to her dimly "painful" sense (246). Chapter 42 almost blatantly provides us with this key. Carrie, literally hugging herself and rejoicing at her good luck in getting a line, comes home to "Hurstwood who, by his presence, caused her merry thoughts to flee and replaced them with *sharp longings for an end of distress*" (314; my italics). Hurstwood has taken on the same aura as the Hanson flat. He is now the repressive rather than the expansive force. He represents and is associated with darkness rather than light. Dreiser then transfers Carrie's interest to Ames immediately: Ames represents the "kindly superiority" that will move Carrie (315). Carrie's courage to climb makes her eligible to benefit from contact with Ames more than it causes her to yearn for him as a lover. Thus, when Hurstwood has come to represent the fear of illness and poverty that dominated Carrie at the very beginning, Ames is brought on as a representative of intellect, much in the same way that Hurstwood had earlier represented passion, love, and marriage in place of Drouet's evasive philandering.

Ames later returns to New York and to Carrie's life when, in counterpoint, Hurstwood is fraught with illness and decline, and Drouet reveals Hurstwood's theft to Carrie. Again, "There was nothing responsive between them" as Carrie and Ames meet, because he thinks her married (354). Nevertheless, he chides her for not going into higher art—"comedy-drama"—and sets "The old call of the ideal" sounding (354). As well, listening to sad music, they are "touched by the same feeling, only hers reached her through the heart" (355). Here, again, a man associates himself with Carrie but not in Carrie's terms. Although Ames is at a higher level than Hurstwood and Drouet, he is not necessarily closer to Carrie, who does not know what it is in his face that appeals to her (354–55). Giving her what she "craved," Ames critiques her face as "a natural expression of its [the world's] longing" (356), but even here, significantly, the novel states, "He was so interested in forwarding all good causes that he sometimes became enthusiastic, giving vent to these preachments. Something in Carrie appealed to him. He wanted to stir her up" (357). Dreiser goes on to describe Ames as "roiling helpless waters," suggesting the extent to which this new lover's comments are as divorced from Carrie's spiritual needs as were the attentions of Drouet and Hurstwood before him. He is one of a chain of admirers fascinated by Carrie's mystery, but coming to it from his own "preachments"—a notably awkward word that suggests his coldness and dry distance.

Carrie's men converge in the climactic moment that unites all four lovers in chapter 46, where Carrie encounters Drouet, then Hurstwood, then Ames in close succession. The sequence immediately follows the moment of Hurstwood's deepest decline through illness to a charity case in chapter 45, "Curious Shifts of the Poor." First Drouet forces himself, through his sheer bluff and good nature, into the backstage area where he finds Carrie, who has just returned to Broadway after a summer away. Carrie is compelled to see him out of courtesy and the dictates of her good nature "for one who had always liked her" (350). She uncomfortably agrees to meet him for dinner the following day. Drouet, as self-centered and good-humored as he was early in the novel, cannot respond to Carrie's altered state except to wish that he can have her again. Yet the feeling of "good nature," a term used repeatedly by Dreiser, dominates. The most significant outcome of the dinner, however, is Drouet's revelation to Carrie that Hurstwood stole $10,000 in Chicago. With this revelation, Carrie feels "instead of hatred springing up there was a kind of sorrow generated" (351). As Drouet rekindles his enthusiasm for Carrie "the all-desirable," the love object is recalled to a broader sympathy with Hurstwood's condition and is more wistfully distanced from men than ever.

Only a handful of sentences after Carrie and Drouet have left the table, Dreiser brings Carrie face to face with the ravaged Hurstwood: shabby, baggy, frightening, and almost unrecognizable after his illness. A more awesome specter than that which haunted her during her dinner with Ames and the Vances in chapter 32, Hurstwood begs money "peevishly, almost resenting her excessive pity," and both fail to connect with one another owing to the "strain of publicity" (352). The "conspicuity" (84) that Hurstwood had feared from the first, and which provided the fatal vulnerability (94, 140), now precludes his chance of receiving help in adversity. As much as ever, their actions are controlled by exterior human forces. Hurstwood shuffles away without revealing his address, thus both acknowledging his change in status and the harshness not of Carrie but of fate: "He seemed to resent her kindly inquiries—so much better had fate dealt with her" (352). That the "apparition" is a "drag on her soul" for days hardly bears out the charge of coldness or ingratitude that some critics level at Carrie. Drouet is treated coldly, however, for in the second and third sentences of the paragraph that the "apparition" sentence initiates, Dreiser concludes, "Drouet called again, but now he was not even seen by her. His attentions seemed out of place." Drouet's attentions are out of place as much because of the greater looming tragedy of Hurstwood's ghost as because Carrie has risen above her need for his financial support.

Ames's reappearance completes our understanding. When Carrie leaves for London: "Both he [Hurstwood] and Drouet were left to discover" her departure, Drouet concluding "at last" that "the old days had gone for good" and Hurstwood "shifted by curious means" through the summer and into the "dead" of winter, when he does not even see the firesigns announcing Carrie's return (353). Drouet "saw it, but did not venture in." Dreiser again enforces the continuity of the three male lovers by following in the next line with the flat announcement "About this time Ames returned to New York." At this time, Carrie is uninterested in Ames because he no longer represents something she does not have. Yet his comments on her acting potential reawaken her yearnings for an unnamed something better—the call of the wild (354). As Drouet is assigned the word "old" as a butterfly, so Carrie's yearning is designated "old" to suggest an inescapable repeating pattern by the same word. Carrie's loneliness deserts her only because Ames takes her seriously, not because he loves her. Yet Dreiser uses the language of seduction as he does when Carrie has her first dinner with Drouet in Chicago; Carrie is delighted, then "wholly aroused," "longing to be equal to this feeling," which "unlocked the door to a new desire" (355–56). Ames's value in the novel is that he allows the reader to assess Carrie as no more analytical, in fact, than she is crassly materialistic; her responses are on an emotional plane.

Seeing in Carrie a representation of the world's longing, Ames is "so interested in forwarding all good causes" that he ends up preaching to her. This leads to his magnifying in Carrie the sadness that derives from the ghost of her previous loves. His asking her to change returns her to her rocking chair: "Still, she did nothing—grieving. It was a long way to this better thing—or seemed so—and comfort was about her; hence the inactivity and longing" (357). These phrases place Carrie in a parallel position to Hurstwood at his most pathetic (295, 315, 318, 321). Seemingly painting Carrie a materialist, Dreiser has carefully retained Hurstwood, weather-beaten and gaunt, just outside this scope. The following chapter, directly following this sentence, returns us to him through an examination of New York's charities for the impoverished. Dreiser, with characteristic ambiguity, has given Carrie greater possibility in Ames's eyes than in her own, and he has left readers aware not only of the alternate viewpoints but also of a broader emotional context developed through the interplay of all of the lovers.

The only further reference to Ames in the 1900 text is Carrie's reading *Père Goriot* on Ames's recommendation, from which she turns to sadly regarding the fate of the poor in the snowstorm in a wistful scene sometimes misinterpreted by critics as suggesting her callousness. Dreiser wrote of Balzac elsewhere that "He it was who pictured . . . the lover, the miser and the innate vagaries of the woman's heart. He knew what hunger means, what cold, and what shabby clothes to the proud heart."[4] Notably, the Balzac novel is a tale of familial abandonment, like Carrie's abandonment of Hurstwood, who is close to his final moment as the snow falls. Nevertheless, Hurstwood takes himself away from Carrie as much as she leaves him. The awareness of Hurstwood's burden of guilt comes to Carrie too late to have a significant impact on their separation and its consequences. Yet Dreiser's intrusion of it so late in the text is clearly intended to suggest to the reader that it might have caused Carrie to reach out to him more actively.

In the Pennsylvania text, Ames is treated as a potential lover, but not necessarily as a solution to Carrie's life. His scientific career is in opposition to Hurstwood just as Hurstwood's saloon manager's role was finer than Drouet's mode of dress and drummer status. This contrast is the basis of a lengthy passage that was cut along with other later Ames material in which Hurstwood is subjected to strict psychological analysis. Echoing Gates's theories, Dreiser writes that Hurstwood was "a fit case for scientific investigation. A splendid paper might be prepared on the operation of preconceived notions which he had concerning dignity in the matter of his downfall" (Penn, 407). The passage continues to make unflattering allusions to the "common canary" and the "house-dog" (Penn, 407). So Hurstwood has lost the "art of shifting and doing" and "courage," qualities that Dreiser forces into his depiction of Ames, even though these qualities have little to do with his actions in the novel. The "poor brain" of Hurstwood, like Drouet's shiny shoes earlier, is established as a foil for Ames.

The Pennsylvania edition chapter in which Ames and Carrie have their lengthy conversation about Carrie's goals on the stage is significantly expanded from the 1900 text. Carrie gazes into Ames's eyes, shades her own "irrepressible feelings" with her lashes, and is hurled into a new round of longing. Ames, for his part, is "wide awake to her beauty," reverses aversions to Carrie's occupation and "moral status," and finds her "exceedingly human and unaffected" (Penn, 486–87). Clearly, the door is opened for the development of a marital or sexual liaison. Ames still has the quality of preaching, looking at Carrie "only in an intellectual way" (Penn, 485), with "the speculative contemplation of the ideal" (Penn, 484), which is his most notable drive. Again, a reader might wonder if he is more fitted than Carrie's previous lovers to understanding the personality of a woman who has been most notable for her craving for the pleasure of being loved.[5]

Each of the loves of Sister Carrie represents an expanded stage of her desire. Ellen Moers has made a strong point about the alternate title of *Sister Carrie*, "The Flesh and the Spirit," suggesting that Gates's scientific theories were providing Dreiser with a philosophical means of literary naturalism (Moers 1969, 167). According to this theory, the state of the mind influences the body, which in turn influences the whole individual. To accept this, however, is not to suggest that the inclusion of Ames as a lover adds anything other than another stage in an already established progression of longing including Drouet and Hurstwood. Whether Ames's role is strengthened, as in the Pennsylvania edition, or left attenuated, as in the 1900 text, the point remains much the same. If anything, the fact that Drouet, more successful, is also very much a presence in the restored Pennsylvania text confirms our feeling that the world will continue on much in the same terms as originally defined, diminishing Hurstwood's power as a character of tragic proportions and giving the novel more of an epic quality paralleling Frank Norris's achievements in *McTeague* and *The Octopus*.

The outcome of *Sister Carrie* is a natural consequence of the socially induced longings on the characters. There is no differentiation between love and yearning in the novel. The characters are impelled by forces and are self-deluding through their own weakness of will. The stronger will of an Ames may lecture the conscience of a Carrie, but he is not likely to bring her peace or fulfillment because of the very undifferentiated nature of her longings. The world is a progression from a low level of material deprivation to higher levels of less material deprivation, but *Sister Carrie* is still a novel about failure. The characters will ever fail to reach the full potential for which they yearn. As such, all of their efforts, as Dreiser impresses on us again and again in the plotting, style, metaphors, and characters, can end only in a tragic failure through blind aspiration. The chief characters are overcome by fatalistic social forces embodied within themselves and the larger world's material expectations represented through their aspirations, and so Dreiser forged the tragedy of *Sister Carrie*.

Notes and References

Chapter 1

1. George Pope Morris, "The Song of the Sewing Machine," in *The Poems of George Pope Morris*, 3d ed. (New York: Scribner, 1860), 202–3. Morris's optimistic praise of the sewing machine as an iron blessing "born to toil and not to feel" was an answer to Thomas Hood's "The Song of the Shirt" in 1842 complaining of the unremitting toil of the poor seamstresses facing starvation.

2. To borrow an idea from Frederick Lewis Allen's *Only Yesterday*.

3. George Horace Lorimer became editor of *The Saturday Evening Post* in 1899 and by 1901 had made the theme of business success the motif of the magazine, bringing the magazine to preeminence among American magazines for 50 years. Lorimer's *Letters from a Self-Made Merchant to His Son*, begun in 1901 and published to instantaneous success as a book in 1902, were the chief examples of the genre that represented the upward aspirations of the lower middle class in this period.

Chapter 2

1. Burton Rascoe, *Theodore Dreiser* (New York: Robert M. McBride & Co., 1925), 28–34; hereafter cited in the text.

2. Dorothy Dudley, *Dreiser and the Land of the Free* (New York: Beechhurst Press, 1946), 181; hereafter cited in the text.

Chapter 3

1. Henry Mills Alden's review for *Harper's Monthly* is photographically reproduced in James L. W. West III, *A "Sister Carrie" Portfolio* (Charlottesville: Bibliography Society of the University of Virginia, 1985), 47. The typist's

note to Dreiser is reproduced on page 27; see also Richard Lingeman, *Theodore Dreiser: At the Gates of the City, 1871–1907* (New York: G.P. Putnam's Sons, 1986), 273.

2. Jack Salzman, ed., *Theodore Dreiser: The Critical Reception* (New York: David Lewis, 1972).

3. Omaha *Daily Bee*, 22 December 1900, reprinted in Salzman, *The Critical Reception*, 5.

4. George Horton, "Strong Local Novel," Chicago *Times-Herald*, 16 January 1901, reprinted in Salzman, *The Critical Reception*, 10.

5. *The Interior*, 21 February 1901, reprinted in Salzman, *The Critical Reception*, 13.

6. *Life*, 24 November 1900, reprinted in Salzman, *The Critical Reception*, 2.

7. George Seibel, Pittsburgh *Commercial Gazette*, 28 December 1900, reprinted in Salzman, *The Critical Reception*, 5.

8. William Marion Reedy, "*Sister Carrie*: A Strangely Strong Novel in a Queer Milieu," St. Louis *Mirror*, 3 January 1901, reprinted in Salzman, *The Critical Reception*, 7.

9. W. A. Swanberg, *Dreiser* (New York: Charles Scribner's Sons, 1965), 91; hereafter cited in the text.

10. London *Daily Mail*, 13 August 1901, reprinted in Salzman, *The Critical Reception*, 18; Manchester *Guardian*, 14 August 1901, reprinted in Salzman, *The Critical Reception*, 19.

11. "Fiction: *Sister Carrie*," *Academy*, 24 August 1901, 153, reprinted in Salzman, *The Critical Reception*, 20.

12. Theodore Watts-Dunton, *Athenaeum*, 7 September 1901, reprinted in Salzman, *The Critical Reception*, 24.

13. New Orleans *Picayune*, 1 July 1907, reprinted in Salzman, *The Critical Reception*, 44.

14. Joseph Horner Coates, " 'Sister Carrie,' " *North American Review* 186 (October 1907): 288–91, reprinted in Salzman, *The Critical Reception*, 51.

15. See Thomas P. Riggio, "Notes on the Origins of *Sister Carrie*," *Library Chronicle* 44 (Spring 1979): 7–26.

16. Akron *Journal*, 30 November 1907, reprinted in Salzman, *The Critical Reception*, 51.

17. Stuart P. Sherman, "The Barbaric Naturalism of Mr. Dreiser," *Nation*, 2 December 1915, reprinted in *The Stature of Theodore Dreiser*, ed. Alfred Kazin and Charles Shapiro (Bloomington: Indiana University Press, 1955), 71–80.

Notes and References

18. Stuart P. Sherman, "Are You Alive?" *Nation*, 1922, reprinted in *The Reader's Digest Twentieth Anniversary Anthology* (Pleasantville, N.Y.: Reader's Digest, 1941), 5–7.

19. Charles C. Baldwin, *The Men Who Make Our Novels* (New York: Dodd, Mead, 1919; rev. ed., 1924), 141.

20. Fred L. Pattee, *The New American Literature, 1890–1930* (New York: Century Co., 1930); hereafter cited in the text.

21. F. O. Matthiessen, *Theodore Dreiser* (New York: Dell, 1950).

22. Manny Farber, "Films," *Nation* 174, 17 May 1952, 485–86.

23. W. A. Swanberg, *Dreiser* (New York: Charles Scribner's Sons, 1965) and Richard Lingeman, *Theodore Dreiser: At the Gates of the City, 1871–1907* (New York: G.P. Putnam's Sons, 1986); hereafter cited in the text.

24. Donald Pizer, *The Novels of Theodore Dreiser: A Critical Study* (Minneapolis: University of Minnesota Press, 1970); Ellen Moers, *Two Dreisers* (New York: Viking Press, 1969); hereafter cited in the text.

Chapter 4

1. James Lundquist, *Theodore Dreiser* (New York: Frederick Unger, 1974), offers one succinct recounting of this event. Dreiser in *Dawn* (New York: Horace Liveright, 1931), 465, recorded his feelings on the subject.

2. "My Brother Paul," in *Twelve Men* (New York: Boni & Liveright, 1919), 76–109; hereafter cited in the text as *Twelve Men*.

3. Documents relating to the case are reprinted in the Norton Critical Edition and Richard Lingeman and other biographers give brief accounts of this incident, close as it is to the nature of the novel. See Lingeman, *Theodore Dreiser*, 66–68, 153–55.

4. This information is derived from Thomas P. Riggio's excellent article "Notes on the Origins of *Sister Carrie*," *Library Chronicle* 44 (Spring 1979): 7–26, part of the issue's symposium on *Sister Carrie*. See also the biographies by Swanberg (113) and Lingeman (244, 394, 396).

5. "The Curious Shifts of the Poor," *Demorest's Family Magazine* 36 (November 1899): 22–26, reprinted in the Norton Critical Edition, 403–12.

6. *Sister Carrie*, Norton Critical Edition, ed. Donald Pizer (New York: W.W. Norton, 1991[1970]), 412; hereafter page numbers are cited in the text.

7. For an interesting comparable treatment of Monroe, see Norman Mailer, *Marilyn* (New York: Perigee Books, 1973).

8. Thomas E. Hill, *Hill's Manual of Social and Business Forms* (Chicago: Hill Standard Book Co., 1884); hereafter cited in the text.

9. Dick Maple, *"He Demons" . . . and . . . "She Devils"* (St. Louis: Standard Book House, 1903); hereafter cited in the text.

141

10. Cathy Davidson and Arnold Davidson, "Carrie's Sisters: The Popular Prototypes of Dreiser's Heroine," *Modern Fiction Studies* 23, no. 3 (Autumn 1977): 396–407; hereafter cited in the text.

11. Notebook entry for Saturday, 14 February 1903, reprinted in *American Diaries, 1902–1926*, ed. Thomas P. Riggio (Philadelphia: University of Pennsylvania Press, 1983), 108–9.

12. Arthur Henry, *A Princess of Arcady* (New York: Doubleday, Page & Co., 1900), 136.

13. Arthur Henry, *An Island Cabin* (New York: McClure, Phillips & Co., 1902), 75.

14. *Sister Carrie*, ed. James L. W. West III et al. (Philadelphia: University of Pennsylvania Press, 1981), 535; hereafter cited in the text as Penn.

15. The discussion here is a much condensed indication of the admirable essay by James L. W. West III, John C. Berkey, and Alice Winters under the title "Historical Commentary," in the University of Pennsylvania edition of *Sister Carrie*, 505–35. Particular reference is made here to discussions on pages 520–22, 532–35, and to later comments on page 583 in the section on "Editorial Principles." The table of deleted passages rejoined to the text is given on pages 661–69, with other "Selected Emendations in the Copy-text" registered at pages 593–635.

16. Dreiser's articles on the strike and a building described in the sort of "walled-city" language that figures Hurstwood's sense of Carrie's stardom from the Toledo *Blade* of March 1894, are reprinted in *Theodore Dreiser Journalism. Volume One, Newspaper Writings, 1892–1895*, ed. T. D. Nostwich (Philadelphia: University of Pennsylvania Press, 1988), 269–77; hereafter cited in the text.

Chapter 5

1. Thanks to Shelley Fisher Fishkin for pointing out the constancy of the fallen woman theme from Susanna Rowson and Hannah Webster Foster's *The Coquette* up to the period under consideration. The actual note as sent through Anna T. Mallon, dated 22 March 1900, is reprinted in West, *A Sister Carrie Portfolio*, 27.

2. These comments are based on the documentation provided in George J. Becker's *Documents of Modern Realism* (Princeton, N.J.: Princeton University Press, 1963).

3. Swanberg, *Dreiser* (92), cites the incident as occurring in the *Harper's Monthly* office in 1900 although his source, Dudley, *Dreiser and the Land of the Free* (197), appears to place it in 1902.

4. The Norton Critical Edition reprints several of these newspaper reports in its section on Background and Sources.

5. Rev. T. De Witt Talmage, *The Abominations of Modern Society* (New York: Adams, Victor & Co., 1872), 94–113; hereafter cited in the text.

6. Pizer, *The Novels of Theodore Dreiser* (32–34) covers the case and its implications for the novel succinctly. The Norton Critical Edition of the novel includes a series of newspaper pieces on the "elopement" of Emma and Hopkins that is informative (374–84).

7. A. H. Hill, *John Smith's Funny Adventures on a Crutch* (Philadelphia: John E. Potter & Co., 1869), 237.

8. George S. McWatters, *Knots Untied; or, Ways and By-Ways in the Hidden Life of American Detectives* (Hartford and Chicago: J.G. Burr & Co., 1874), 131–52.

9. Sandy Petrey, "The Language of Realism, the Language of False Consciousness: A Reading of *Sister Carrie*," *Novel* 10, no. 2 (Winter 1977): 107; hereafter cited in the text.

10. Walter Benn Michaels, "*Sister Carrie*'s Popular Economy," *Critical Inquiry* 7, no. 2 (Winter 1980); 387–88.

Chapter 6

1. Reprinted in Nostwich, *Theodore Dreiser Journalism*, 269–77.

2. 2. vols., ed. Yoshinobu Hakutani (Rutherford, N.J.: Fairleigh Dickinson University Press, 1987).

3. Ellen Moers, "The Finesse of Dreiser," *American Scholar* 33 (1963): 111; hereafter cited in the text.

4. Edith Wharton, *The Custom of the Country* (New York: Scribner's, 1913), chap. 10.

5. James L. W. West III, "John Paul Dreiser's Copy of *Sister Carrie*," *Library Chronicle* 44, no. 1 (Spring 1979): 85–93.

6. Arun Mukherjee, *The Gospel of Wealth in the American Novel* (Totowa, N.J.: Barnes & Noble, 1987), 18–21, 118–19.

7. Lawrence Hussman, *Dreiser and His Fiction* (Philadelphia: University of Pennsylvania Press, 1983), 38–39.

8. Henry Nash Smith, in "A Textbook of the Genteel Tradition: Henry Ward Beecher's *Norwood*," in *Democracy in the Novel* (New York: Oxford University Press, 1978), 56–74, contends about Beecher's readers, similarly, that they bought the book expecting to read Beecher's philosophical address to them, but Beecher's reputation was established at the time of his novel's publication as Dreiser's was not.

9. Phillip Williams, "The Chapter Titles of *Sister Carrie*," *American Literature* 36 (1964): 359–65.

Chapter 7

1. Frequently anthologized, this essay first appeared in *Booklovers Magazine*, 1 (February 1903): 129; it is reprinted in George J. Becker, *Documents of Modern Literary Realism* (Princeton, N.J.: Princeton University Press, 1963), 154–56, which includes a useful note and also the Sherman essay "The Barbaric Naturalism of Mr. Dreiser," and in the Norton Critical Edition.

2. Philip Fisher, "The Life History of Objects: The Naturalist Novel in the City," in *Hard Facts: Setting and Form in the American Novel* (New York: Oxford University Press, 1985), 5–7, 12–14; hereafter cited in the text.

3. Edward W. Bok, "A Country Lad in the City," in *A Practical Book for Practical People* (Springfield, Mass.: King-Richardson Publishing Co., 1896), 275.

4. *Selected Poems of Thomas Hardy*, ed. John Crowe Ransom (New York: Macmillan, 1961), 26–27.

5. Eliseo Vivas contends this particularly strongly in "Dreiser, An Inconsistent Mechanist" reprinted in Kazin and Shapiro, *The Stature of Theodore Dreiser*, 237–45; see especially page 242.

6. Theodore Dreiser to John Howard Lawson, advising about a play based on *Sister Carrie*, 10 October 1928, reprinted in the Norton Critical Edition of *Sister Carrie*, 475–76.

7. Fisher, *Hard Facts* (3–21), reaches a similar conclusion connecting Cooper as a writer of the frontier, Stowe as a writer of the domestic setting, and Dreiser as a writer of the cityscape.

Chapter 8

1. See Suvir Kaul, "Why Selima Drowns: Thomas Gray and the Domestication of the Imperial Ideal," *PMLA* 105, no. 2 (March 1990): 223–32.

2. Johnston Smith [Stephen Crane], *Maggie, A Girl of the Streets (A Story of New York)* (New York: n.p., 1893), 41.

3. *Demorest's Monthly Magazine* 22, no. 9 (July 1886): 579–83.

Chapter 9

1. Bertil C. Nelson, "William James' Concept of Self and the Fictive Psychology of Theodore Dreiser in *Sister Carrie*," in *Essays in Arts and Sciences* 19 (1990): 56–57.

2. John C. Hirsh, "The Printed Ephemera of *Sister Carrie*," *American Literary Realism, 1870–1910* 7, no. 2 (Spring 1974): 171–72, has noted

how the novel is "charged" with the ephemera of the time, particularly the newspaper, with its floods of intelligence of the bright and beautiful, and subsequently awful world.

3. Lawrence E. Hussman, "Thomas Edison and *Sister Carrie*: A Source for Character and Theme," *American Literary Realism: 1870–1910* 8, no. 2 (Spring 1975): 155–58, notes that Dreiser had interviewed Edison for *Success* magazine a year before he met Gates and was much impressed by the inventor's indifference to money, emphasis on inborn talent and hard work, broad forehead, and other characteristics that are prominent in the description of Bob Ames, particularly in the manuscript version of the novel. Dreiser's article on Edison is reprinted in Hakutani, *Selected Magazine Articles of Theodore Dreiser*, vol. 2: 111–19. Dreiser wrote about Edison: "In the rush of the metropolis, a man finds his true level without delay, especially when his talents are of so practical and brilliant a nature as were this young telegrapher's" (2: 116). The phrasing is suggestive of the treatment of all the main figures in the novel. Moers and Lingeman also discuss the influence of Gates extensively in their respective books.

4. "Balzac" is reprinted in *Theodore Dreiser: A Selection of Uncollected Prose*, ed. Donald Pizer (Detroit: Wayne State University Press, 1977), 59.

5. William J. Burling, " 'The Feast of Belshazzar' and *Sister Carrie*," *American Literary Realism: 1870–1910* 17, no. 1 (Spring 1984): 40–43, reaches the same conclusion in examining the deleted last half of a chapter title for chapter 32, " 'The Feast of Belshazzar': A Seer to Translate. A Second Look at the Ambassador's Credentials."

Selected Bibliography

Primary Works

Editions of *Sister Carrie*

The first American edition of *Sister Carrie* was published by Doubleday, Page & Co., New York, 1900. William Heinemann, London, published an edition in 1901 in its "Dollar Library" with major cuts by Arthur Henry. B. W. Dodge & Co., New York, published an edition for Dreiser in 1907 with only the passage cribbed from George Ade altered and the dedication to Arthur Henry removed. Constable in London published an edition in 1927, unabridged, and the Heritage Press published an edition for the Limited Editions Club in New York in 1939 with an introduction by Burton Rascoe and illustrations by Reginald Marsh. The Modern Library, New York, published an edition in 1932 with a brief commentary on *Sister Carrie*'s history by Dreiser.

Pizer, Donald ed. Norton Critical Edition, New York: W.W. Norton, 1991 [1970]. The 1900 Doubleday, Page text, including valuable contemporary writings by Dreiser, some of the correspondence surrounding the 1900 "suppression," and a useful selection of major critical appraisals through the 1950s. The second edition printed in 1991 also carries a useful table of cuts and emendations relating to the original manuscript.

West, James L. W. III, John C. Berkey, and Alice M. Winters, *eds.* Philadelphia: University of Pennsylvania Press, 1981. Known as the Pennsylvania edition, this printing of the novel restores hundreds of textual words and passages from the original manuscript that were deleted or altered by Dreiser on Arthur Henry's and Jug's recommendations or by copy editors at Doubleday. Two hundred pages of textual apparatus and historical discussion by West and historical editors John C. Berkey and Alice M. Winters document changes and provide alternate passages; users should be cautioned that changes made in proof—some significant—are not listed in indexes of changes printed with the new text.

Selected Bibliography

Merrill Standard Edition. Columbus, Ohio: Charles E. Merrill Pub. Co., 1969. A facsimile reproduction of the 1900 Doubleday, Page edition with an introduction by Louis Auchincloss.

Penguin Classics edition. New York: Penguin Books, 1981. The 1981 Pennsylvania text with a brief introduction by Alfred Kazin but without the supporting textual apparatus.

Signet Classic edition. New York: Signet, 1980. The 1900 text with a brief afterword by Willard Thorp.

Other Works

Free and Other Stories. New York: Boni & Liveright, 1918. Includes "Free," "McEwen of the Shining Slave Makers," "Nigger Jeff," and "Old Rogaum and His Theresa," bearing on *Sister Carrie.*

A Gallery of Women. 2 vols. New York: Horace Liveright, 1929. Further insights into Dreiser's views of women.

Letter of Theodore Dreiser: A Selection. Edited by Robert H. Elias. Philadelphia: University of Pennsylvania Press, 1959. Contains selected letters relating to the publication of *Sister Carrie.*

Selected Magazine Articles of Theodore Dreiser. 2 vols. Edited by Yoshinobu Hakutani. Rutherford, N.J.: Fairleigh Dickinson University Press, 1985. Prose writings from the 1890s for popular magazines.

Theodore Dreiser Journalism. Volume 1, Newspaper Writings, 1892–1895. Edited by T. D. Nostwich. Philadelphia: University of Pennsylvania Press, 1988. A collection of newspaper writing from 1892 through 1895, including the 1894 Toledo streetcar strike. A second volume in the series is now in preparation by Shelley Fisher Fishkin.

Theodore Dreiser: A Selection of Uncollected Prose. Edited by Donald Pizer. Detroit: Wayne State University Press, 1977. A wide-ranging selection of newspaper and magazine writing from 1892 on, including a number of pieces pertinent to *Carrie.*

Twelve Men. New York: Boni and Liveright, 1918. Includes analysis of brother Paul, which may underlie Hurstwood's portrayal.

Secondary Works

Biographies

Dudley, Dorothy. *Dreiser and the Land of the Free.* New York: Beechhurst Press, 1946. Originally published in 1932 as *Forgotten Frontiers: Dreiser and the Land of the Free.* A somewhat melodramatized vision of Dreiser as a pioneer of modernism in the new world of science and machinery, with considerable material based on Dreiser's own impressions; blames Mrs. Doubleday for the suppression of the novel.

Elias, Robert. *Theodore Dreiser: Apostle of Nature.* New York: Alfred Knopf, 1949. A standard and reliable biography.

Lingeman, Richard. *Theodore Dreiser: At the Gates of the City, 1871–1907.* New York: G. P. Putnam's Sons, 1986. A detailed and readable study of the background and writing of *Sister Carrie,* including secondary interests such as Paul Dresser's popular songs, Steiglitz's photography, and other contemporary materials, along with intelligent commentary on the novel.

Lundquist, James. *Theodore Dreiser.* New York: Frederic Unger, 1974.

Matthiessen, F. O. *Theodore Dreiser.* New York: Dell, 1950.

Rascoe, Burton. *Theodore Dreiser.* New York: Robert M. McBride & Company, 1925. Treats Dreiser as the great epic American novelist, inspired by his experience in Pittsburgh and his reading of Balzac to turn to a serious portrayal of the new industrial world and its morality.

Shapiro, Charles. *Theodore Dreiser: Our Bitter Patriot.* Carbondale: Southern Illinois University Press, 1962.

Swanberg, W. A. *Dreiser.* New York: Charles Scribner's Sons, 1965. Generally accepted as the authoritative biography of Dreiser's life.

Criticism: Books

Gerber, Philip L. *Theodore Dreiser.* New York: Twayne Publishers, 1964. A brief, intelligent introduction to the author with about 30 pages on *Carrie.*

Kazin, Alfred, and Charles Shapiro, eds. *The Stature of Theodore Dreiser.* Bloomington: Indiana University Press, 1955. A comprehensive collection of critical commentary on Dreiser including, among others, important essays by Edgar Lee Masters, Sherwood Anderson, Stuart P. Sherman, H. L. Mencken, F. O. Matthiessen, C. C. Walcutt, as well as Malcolm Cowley and James T. Farrell on *Sister Carrie* specifically.

Lehan, Richard. *Theodore Dreiser, His World and His Novels.* Carbondale: Southern Illinois University Press, 1969. Includes a chapter on *Sister Carrie* with some provocative clearly stated judgments.

Moers, Ellen. *Two Dreisers.* New York: Viking Press, 1969. A thorough-going study of sources, milieu, and philosophy as leading to and finally embodied in the texts of *Sister Carrie* and *An American Tragedy.*

Mukherjee, Arun. *The Gospel of Wealth in the American Novel.* Totowa, N.J.: Barnes & Noble Books, 1987. A helpful and informative discussion of the "Knights and Pilgrims" imagery expropriated by American business apologists in the nineteenth century and a useful application of the findings to *Sister Carrie* and other Dreiser novels.

Pizer, Donald. *The Novels of Theodore Dreiser, A Critical Study.* Minneapolis: University of Minnesota Press, 1976. Includes a lengthy and detailed analysis of Dreiser's method using the symbolic motifs of heat/cold and the rocking chair to show how the pursuit of human warmth estranges human beings from each other.

Salzman, Jack, ed. *Theodore Dreiser: The Critical Reception.* New York: David Lewis, 1972. Reprints large numbers of reviews of all of Dreiser's major works, including about 70 reviews of *Carrie* from 1900–1901 and 1907, along with helpful introductory commentary by the editor.

West, James L. W. III. *A Sister Carrie Portfolio.* Charlottesville: Bibliographical Society of the University of Virginia, 1985. A visual companion to the 1981 Pennsylvania edition that gives many photographs relating to Dreiser and the page-by-page manuscript revisions, as well as related historical and background materials.

Criticism: Articles

Brennan, Stephen C. "The Two Endings of *Sister Carrie*." *Studies in American Fiction* 16, no. 1 (Spring 1988): 13–26. Argues the choice of endings in the Pennsylvania edition, suggesting that Dreiser's revisions show a high degree of self-awareness about his own marital discomfort.

Davidson, Cathy N. and Arnold E. "Carrie's Sisters: The Popular Prototypes of Dreiser's Heroine." *Modern Fiction Studies* 23, no. 3 (Autumn 1977): 395–407. A convincing study of *Sister Carrie's* deviations from the sentimental romances of the 1870–1900 period most clearly embodied in Laura Jean Libbey's *Little Leafy* (1891) and Bertha M. Clay's *Dora Thorne* (1883) with their conventional marriage-oriented plots and sentimentally pure heroines. Included in a symposium issue on Dreiser.

Fisher, Philip. "The Life History of Objects: The Naturalist Novel in the City" in *Hard Facts: Setting and Form in the American Novel*; 128–179. New York: Oxford University Press, 1985. The city models the larger society, establishing a basis for the hollowness of characters, their sale of self, and their decline in various images.

Hayes, Kevin. "Textual Anomalies in the 1900 Doubleday, Page *Sister Carrie. American Literary Realism, 1870–1910* 22, no. 1 (Fall 1989): 53–68. A strongly stated critical defense of the Pennsylvania edition over the 1900 text on the grounds that the revision "eliminates discontinuities and improves the coherence of the novel," based on close study of logical antecedents and stylistic elements.

Mencken, H. L. "Theodore Dreiser." *A Book of Prefaces*, 67–148. New York: Alfred A. Knopf, 1917. Despite being written early in Dreiser's career, still one of the shrewdest and most rounded critical appraisals of Dreiser, placing the "tangled complex of striving and aspiration" of Carrie in relation to the growing rejection by Dreiser of the "appeal to facile sentiment" in later works.

Michaels, Walter Benn. "*Sister Carrie's* Popular Economy." *Critical Inquiry* 7, no. 2 (Winter 1980): 373–90. A well-reasoned examination of how *Carrie* succeeds Howells's *The Rise of Silas Lapham*, deriving its power from the excesses and disequilibriums that capitalism forces upon Carrie as "desire," the force of which Hurstwood loses.

Moers, Ellen. "The Finesse of Dreiser." *American Scholar* 33 (1963): 109–14. An impressive definition of the "lyrical" and "contrapuntal" effects of language to express the mental attitudes of the inarticulate Carrie, bolstered by a clear and succinct analysis and citation of a passage cut from the manuscript that shows Dreiser's awareness of what he was doing.

Nelson, Bertil C. "William James' Concept of Self and the Fictive Psychology of Theodore Dreiser in *Sister Carrie*." *Essays in Arts and Sciences* 19 (1990): 45–63. William James' concept of self-definition through the balancing of a social, material, and idealistic "Me" is related to the behavior of the chief characters and particularly Hurstwood.

Petrey, Sandy. "The Language of Realism, the Language of False Consciousness: A Reading of *Sister Carrie*." *Novel* 10, no. 2 (Winter 1977): 101–13. An extremely valuable article that contends that the interplay of clearly written reporting with the overdrawn language of bathos and sentiment is crucial in undercutting sentimental posturing and its accompanying myths.

Riggio, Thomas P. "Notes on the Origins of *Sister Carrie*." *Library Chronicle* 44 (Spring 1979): 7–26. A valuable study of the meanings of the idea of sisterhood to Dreiser along with a very useful expansion of our notion of Carrie Rutter, along with her sister Maud, as providing significant models for the atmosphere and personality of Carrie in the novel, not to mention the title.

West, James L. W. III. "*Nicholas Blood* and *Sister Carrie*." *Library Chronicle* 44 (Spring 1979): 32–42. Convincing analysis of March 1902 items in *Bookman* that show Arthur Henry urged Dreiser to resist suppression of his novel because of Henry's previous experience in publishing the earlier work. Also suggests that the material was meant to get Dreiser to revise and expand the Carrie-Ames romance.

Bibliography

Pizer, Donald. *Theodore Dreiser: A Primary and Secondary Bibliography.* Boston: G. K. Hall & Co., 1975.

Selected Bibliography

Historical Sources

(Clay, Bertha M.) Braeme, Charlotte M. *Dora Thorne.* Chicago: M.A. Donahue & Co., n.d. Originally published in 1883, a novel providing Dreiser with an example of the sentimental domestic melodrama that he rejected.

Hill, Thomas E. *Hill's Manual of Social and Business Forms: A Guide to Correct Writing.* Chicago: Hill Standard Book Co., 1884. Given to young Theo by his mother and apparently a source of early reading, this book provides forms of both writing and deportment, representing the ethical ideals of the period.

Maple, Col. Dick. *"He Demons" . . . and . . . "She Devils."* St. Louis, Mo.: Standard Book House, 1903. A lurid exposé of vice intended to appeal to a popular audience of the turn of the century and expressing representative attitudes of a segment of American culture.

Miller, Joaquin. *The Destruction of Gotham.* New York: Funk & Wagnalls, 1886. A significant alternative plot that parallels Dreiser's novel.

Talmage, Rev. T. De Witt. *The Abominations of Modern Society.* New York: Adams, Victor & Co., 1872. Fulminations on the place of men and women in modern urban life by one of America's most popular religious orators of the later nineteenth century.

Index

Index

The Author

David E. E. Sloane is professor of English at the University of New Haven. A specialist in nineteenth-century literature with emphasis on American humor and Mark Twain, he earned his doctorate from Duke University in 1970. His books include *Mark Twain as a Literary Comedian* (1979); *The Literary Humor of the Urban Northeast, 1830–1890* (1982); *American Humor Magazines and Comic Periodicals* (1987); and *Adventures of Huckleberry Finn: American Comic Vision* (1988).